Jane Eyre

Charlotte Brontë

ABOUT YOUR BOOK

MP3	Go to Helbling e-zone to listen to or download the chapter or activity
(headphones icon)	Listen to the chapter
(speech bubbles icon)	Talk about the story
glossary•	When you see the blue dot, check the word in the glossary
P	Prepare for Cambridge English Exams: Preliminary
FACT FILE	Read informative fact files which develop themes from the story
LIFE SKILLS	Make comparisons between the story and contemporary life
e-ZONE	Go to Helbling e-zone to do activities

FOR THE TEACHER

A state-of-the-art interactive learning environment with 1000s of free online self-correcting activities for your chosen readers.

Go to our Readers Resource site for information on using readers and downloadable Resource Sheets, photocopiable Worksheets and Answer Keys. Plus free sample tracks from the story.
helbling.com/readers

For lots of great ideas on using Graded Readers consult Reading Matters, the Teacher's Guide to using Helbling Readers.

Contents

HELBLING DIGITAL

INTERACTIVE ONLINE TEACHING AND LEARNING MATERIALS

e·zone

THE EDUCATIONAL PLATFORM

HELBLING e-zone is an inspiring new state-of-the-art, easy-to-use interactive learning environment.

Use the **personal access code** on the inside front cover of this book to unlock a host of self-correcting activities, including:

- reading comprehension;
- listening comprehension;
- vocabulary;
- grammar;
- exam preparation.

TEACHERS register free of charge to set up classes and assign individual and class homework sets. Results are provided automatically once the deadline has been reached and detailed reports on performance are available at a click.

STUDENTS test their language skills in a stimulating interactive environment. All activities can be attempted as many times as necessary and full results and feedback are given as soon as the deadline has been reached. Single student access is also available.

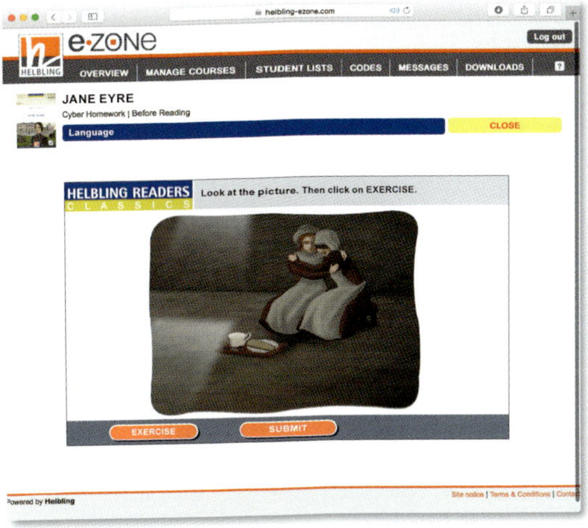

1000s of free online interactive activities now available for HELBLING READERS and your other favourite Helbling Languages publications.

ONLINE ACTIVITIES

helbling-ezone.com

blog.helblingreaders.com

Love reading and readers and can't wait to get your class interested? Have a class library and reading programme but not sure how to take it a step further? The Helbling Readers BLOG is the place for you.

The **Helbling Readers BLOG** will provide you with ideas on setting up and running a Book Club and tips on reading lessons **every week**.

- Book Club
- Worksheets
- Lesson Plans

Subscribe to our **BLOG** and you will never miss out on our updates.

ABOUT THE AUTHOR

Charlotte Brontë was born in 1816. Her father was a clergyman• and the family lived in a parsonage• in Haworth, a small village in Yorkshire, England. Her mother died when she was five and Charlotte and her brother and sisters were brought up• by their aunt. For a short time she attended a school with her older sisters Maria and Elizabeth and her younger sister, Emily. However, when Maria and Elizabeth both died of tuberculosis• in 1825, Charlotte and Emily left the school and were taught at home by their father.

Charlotte worked for a short time as a governess• in Yorkshire, and then went to Brussels to learn French and later to teach there.

On her return to Yorkshire, she tried to open a school in Haworth together with her sisters Emily and Anne. But it was not a success because Haworth was too isolated. Instead she and her sisters turned to• writing.

In 1846 Charlotte persuaded her sisters to publish *Poems by Currer, Ellis and Acton Bell* (the sisters all had pseudonyms• because it was not common for women of the time to be writers). This was a commercial disaster. But in 1847 Charlotte's *Jane Eyre* was published and the book was an immediate success.

In 1854 Charlotte Brontë married Reverend A.B. Nicholls but she died the following year, aged only 39.

- **brought up:** looked after (when a child)
- **clergyman:** priest
- **governess:** woman who lives with a family and teaches their children at home
- **parsonage:** house that the Church of England gives a priest to live in
- **pseudonyms:** names used by writers instead of their own names
- **tuberculosis**: a serious infectious disease
- **turned to:** started

ABOUT THE BOOK

Jane Eyre (1847) is set• in the Yorkshire Dales• in Victorian Britain•. It was not a conventional• novel of the time, but was an immediate success with the reading public and is still popular today.

The book is about growth•, courage and love and tells the story of a poor orphan• girl who grows up in a difficult environment. Jane Eyre's character evolves gradually. The reader can see her passions as a young girl slowly turn to reason as she becomes a more mature and independent woman. For this reason the novel can be seen as a *Bildungsroman*•.

The book is written as a first-person narrative; in this way the reader has direct contact with Jane and her feelings and actions. She comes across as a courageous woman who works hard to change and improve her situation.

After leaving her heartless aunt at Gateshead Hall, Jane Eyre goes to boarding school• at Lowood Institution. She learns to become a governess and gets her first job at Thornfield Hall. Jane soon falls in love with her employer, Mr Rochester. Their love is complicated because of her position as his governess but also for another important reason: a mysterious presence in the attic of Thornfield Hall.

Jane Eyre does not stop loving Mr Rochester but she also wants to be a respected and independent woman. Her choices throughout the novel show her to be a strong and modern heroine of her time and one of the first feminist role models in literature. The novel deals with many themes including women's role in society, family, social class and forgiveness.

- **Bildungsroman:** novel which follows the growth and emotional development of the central character
- **boarding school:** type of school where students live
- **conventional:** traditional or ordinary
- **dales:** hills and valleys
- **growth:** (here) development, both physical and emotional
- **is set:** takes place in
- **orphan:** child with no parents
- **Victorian Britain:** see page 17

WHAT'S SO SPECIAL ABOUT JANE?

A NOVEL OF CONTRASTS

Why does Jane Eyre continue to fascinate modern readers? The intensity of the feelings, the richness of the language, and the powerful representation of passion in its dramatic plot are only some of the reasons. *Jane Eyre* is a very unusual novel, full of contrasts and opposing concepts. Critics have tried to categorize the various conflicting forces in the novel by labelling them passion versus duty, passion versus reason, Romanticism versus Rationalism, Nature versus Christianity, and so on. But these labels are simplistic, because the divisions cut across each other in complex ways. And in *Jane Eyre*, Charlotte Brontë gives voice to these conflicting forces by dramatizing both

sides of each issue. This richness of contrasts and even contradictions is the strength of the book. The novel reflects the history of romantic love in the West, where most often passion is in marked contrast to a Christianized idea of love.

FOLLOWING TRADITION

The novel is both original and yet a direct descendent• of earlier works of literature. On the one hand, Brontë's novel reflects the tendencies of the time and includes various aspects of Victorian fiction. The influence of the Gothic novel is also evident and the author seems to reuse Byronic and Gothic models for the characters of Mr and Mrs Rochester. Last but not least, the novel belongs to yet another kind of narrative, the *Bildungsroman*, or coming of age novel. It follows the main character, from childhood, through a series of trials•, to maturity. *David Copperfield*, *The Mill on the Floss*, and *Great Expectations* are other famous examples of this kind of narrative. Brontë's novel follows a scheme in which education, marriage and motherhood, according to the Victorian view, are all seen as steps in the real purpose of Jane's life.

- **categorize:** organize in separate groups or categories
- **concepts:** ideas
- **cut across:** (here) affect
- **descendant:** (here) linked to the past
- **labelling:** putting names or labels
- **representation:** (here) description
- **simplistic:** too simple
- **trials:** (here) problems
- **versus:** against

AN ORIGINAL VOICE

On the other hand, since its publication in 1847, both critics and public have recognized that the novel is something different. Jane is unlike any other heroine of the period, starting from her plainness of appearance, dress, and manner. The figure of the isolated orphan was a common theme of the time, but other aspects of Jane's personality are highly original. Her confidence and sincerity, her strong determination, her explosions of anger and passion are all aspects which set her apart from the pretty, modest, and respectable woman so common in Victorian fiction. Jane seems to challenge the conventions of gender

roles in romantic love. She doesn't accept the passive and dependent role in romance that women are commonly associated with. She asserts• the right of women to love and be loved as well as being valued as individuals. This too, violated• accepted social codes of femininity and respectability and shocked some of the critics of the time.

LOVE AND IDENTITY

In fact, Jane is a mix of rebellion and traditional values, and towards the end, the novel is at its most ambivalent. Jane rebels against the social and economic inequalities involved in courtship• and marriage in society of the time. But in the end the solution that she chooses is Victorian and traditional. Why? Maybe because she has found out that illegitimate• feelings and desires are threats to social harmony and order, and they do not follow society's ideal of purity and marriage. Romantic passion is not the answer to Jane's search. She wants her idea of love to be accepted within a Christian framework. Brontë seems to suggest that in the end the experience of romantic love is necessary but does not fully make up• a woman's identity. Passion is a way of getting to know oneself better. It is the key to a search for a deeper meaning than the one defined for women by cultural conventions.

- **asserts:** expresses; says
- **challenge:** (here) question; go against
- **conventions:** accepted rules
- **courtship:** period when a couple get to know each other romantically
- **illegitimate:** (here) that are considered wrong
- **make up:** (here) complete
- **manner:** way of acting
- **plainness:** ordinary appearance; lack of beauty
- **set her apart:** make her different
- **violated:** (here) went against

Jane Eyre

Mrs Fairfax

Blanche Ingram

Mrs Rochester

St John Rivers

BEFORE READING

1 **Look at these pictures of Jane Eyre. Match the correct description to each picture.**

- **a** Jane with her cousin in her aunt's home.
- **b** Jane with her friend at boarding school.
- **c** Jane with her pupil when she is a governess.
- **d** Jane with her beloved as an independent woman.

2 **What kind of person do you think Jane Eyre is? Work with a partner and write a list of possible words to describe her.**

3 Jane Eyre is an orphan. Here is a definition of the word 'orphan'.

orphan ['ɔ:fn]
(noun) a child whose parents are dead.

Now write definitions for these words. Use a dictionary if necessary.

a cousins

....

b governess

....

c housekeeper

....

d owner

....

e parents

....

f superintendent

....

g teacher

....

4 Use the words from Exercise 3 to complete the sentences below.

a Jane Eyre works as a .... at Thornfield Hall. Her little ward is called Adela. The ...., Mrs Fairfax, is friendly and kind. Jane meets and gradually falls in love with the .... of the house, Mr Rochester.

b The only nice .... at Lowood is the .... Miss Temple. The owner, Mr Brocklehurst, is very strict.

c When Jane Eyre's .... die she is sent to live with her aunt and uncle and her ....: the Reed family.

BEFORE READING

1 Match the words from the story with the pictures.

slates advertisement stool easel
piano drawing sewing benches

a ☐ 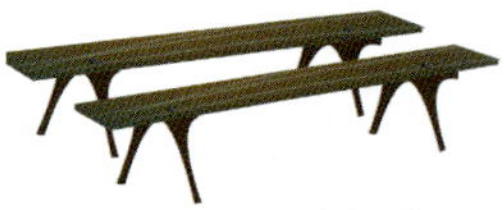

b ☐ 

c ☐ 

d ☐ 

e ☐ 

f ☐ 

g ☐ 

h ☐ 

2 Use each of the words from Exercise 1 to complete the following sentences.

- **a** In the library there was an .... for painting.
- **b** I wanted to look for a new job so I decided to put an .... in the newspaper.
- **c** I was standing on a .... in the middle of the room and everyone was looking at me.
- **d** When Mr Brocklehurst entered the schoolroom everyone stopped writing on their .... and stood up.
- **e** I decided to spend the afternoon doing some .... for Adela's lessons the next day so I went upstairs to get some paper and pencils.
- **f** Grace Poole does the .... and other jobs.
- **g** Girls of all ages were sitting on wooden .... on each side of long tables.
- **h** I heard her invite him to sing while she played the ....

3 Match the words in the box to the numbers in the picture.

on foot open carriage coach on horse

4 Read the following text about Victorian Britain.

The Victorian age in British history is named after Queen Victoria, who was Britain's queen from 1837 until 1901. Life in Victorian times was not the same as it is now. There were big differences in homes, schools, jobs and entertainment. No TV, no computers, no central heating. Transport was very different too. Most people travelled on foot or by coach for longer distances. Only richer people had horses to ride or carriages to go out in. Train travel in the 1840s was still very rare because there weren't many railway lines. There were no cars (until the last few years of Victoria's reign). There was no air travel but only very long journeys on ships.

Work with a partner and write a list of the differences between life now and in Victorian times. Discuss with another pair.

e-ZONE ONLINE ACTIVITIES Before Reading

1 Gateshead Hall

It was raining heavily and very cold outside. My aunt, Mrs Reed, was lying on a sofa in front of the fire in the drawing room•. Her three children Eliza, John, and Georgiana were sitting around her but she didn't want me there.

'Jane, you can sit with us when you become more pleasant,' she said. 'Now go away and be quiet.'

I went into the breakfast room and chose a book from the bookcase•. Then I climbed into the window seat• behind the curtain with it.

Suddenly the door opened.

'Hello!' cried John Reed. Then he paused. He thought the room was empty.

'Where is she?' he continued. 'Lizzy! Georgy! Jane isn't here. Tell mama she's gone out in the rain!'

Eliza put her head round the door. 'She's behind the curtain, John.'

I came out immediately. I didn't want to be pulled out by John.

'What do you want?' I asked.

'Say, "What do you want, Master Reed?"' John answered. He sat down in an armchair and continued, 'I want you to come here.'

John Reed was fourteen – four years older than me and he bullied• me continually. I was very afraid of him. No one in the house took my side•. The servants were too afraid and his mother, Mrs Reed, didn't notice. I was completely alone.

I came up to his chair and he stuck out his tongue at me.

- **bookcase:** 
- **bullied:** hurt and frightened because I was smaller and less powerful
- **drawing room:** comfortable room in a large house used for relaxing
- **took my side:** supported me
- **window seat:** seat below a window

I knew that he wanted to hit me. As I looked at him I thought, 'How ugly you are.'

Maybe he knew what I was thinking because he suddenly lifted his hand and hit me hard. I fell back a step or two from his chair.

'That is for being rude to my mama,' said John, 'and for hiding behind curtains, and for looking at me in that way – you rat!'

I was sure he wanted to hit me again.

'What were you doing behind the curtain?' he demanded.

'I was reading.'

'Show me the book.'

I returned to the window seat and picked up the book.

'You have no right• to take our books. You aren't part of our family. You have no money. Your father left you nothing. You have no right to live here with gentlemen's children like us and eat the same meals that we eat and wear clothes that our mama buys for you. I'll teach you to take my books! Because they are mine. Everything in this house will be mine in a few years. Go and stand by the door.'

I did and John threw the book at me. I fell and hit my head. It started to bleed and was very painful. Suddenly I felt angry.

'Wicked• and cruel• boy!' I said. 'You are like a murderer! You are like the Roman emperors!'

'What! What!' he cried. 'Did you hear her, Eliza and Georgiana? I'll tell mama!'

He ran towards me, grabbed• my hair and shook me. I fought back furiously.

'Rat! Rat!' he shouted.

- **cruel:** very unkind and wanting to cause pain
- **grabbed:** took suddenly and with force
- **have no right:** are not authorised to
- **wicked:** bad

Eliza and Georgiana ran to find Mrs Reed. They came back with Bessie the nurse• and Miss Abbot the maid• behind them.

'Can you believe it? She attacked Master John!' I heard someone say.

'Take her away to the red room,' said Mrs Reed. 'And lock the door.'

Bessie and Miss Abbot took hold of me. I fought them and tried to escape.

'Hold her arms, Miss Abbot,' shouted Bessie. 'She's like a mad cat.'

When we got to the red room, they pushed me onto a chair.

'Sit still or I'll tie your hands,' said Bessie.

'I won't move,' I promised and held the chair with my hands.

They stood and looked at me. Their faces were very serious.

'Don't forget, Miss,' Bessie began, 'that you owe a lot to• Mrs Reed. The only reason that you aren't in the poorhouse• is because she looks after you.'

I didn't reply. The words weren't new to me.

Then Bessie and Miss Abbot left me. They shut the door and locked it behind them.

Jane

What do we know about Jane? Tick (✓) the correct boxes.

- ☐ She is an orphan.
- ☐ She has no money.
- ☐ She is not happy.
- ☐ She is not welcome in the home where she lives.
- ☐ She has a good relationship with her cousins.
- ☐ She is a servant in the house.

- **maid:** (here) woman who works as a servant in someone's house
- **nurse:** (here) woman who takes care of someone's young children
- **owe a lot to:** (here) must thank
- **poorhouse:** building where very poor people could live and eat

The room was cold because it was never used. Mr Reed, my uncle, died in this room nine years ago and everyone believed the room was haunted by his ghost•. I couldn't remember my uncle but I knew that he was my mother's brother. My parents died when I was a baby and Mr Reed took me into his house. Before dying he made Mrs Reed promise to look after me and treat me as one of her own children. Perhaps Mrs Reed tried but she was unable to love me. I wasn't her child and I wasn't pretty or happy. How could I be happy?

I stayed in the red room all night. It was terrible. My mind was full of nightmares and voices. I was so frightened that I fainted•. When they found me in the morning, they called Mr Lloyd the doctor to look at me. He asked me lots of questions. He was a kind man and I told him about my cruel cousin, John Reed, and about my unhappiness. Mr Lloyd listened to my story. Then he asked if he could talk to Mrs Reed. He suggested a solution to everyone's problems. Mrs Reed must send Jane Eyre away to school.

Soon I was well again but nobody in the house talked to me and I was treated worse than before. But things were changing.

November, December, and half of January passed. Christmas and the New Year were celebrated at Gateshead Hall with the usual festive cheer. Everyone exchanged presents and there were lots of dinners and evening parties. I was excluded from all enjoyment of course. In the evenings I sat on the stairs and watched while my cousins had fun. Then I went back to the lonely, silent nursery. I sat looking at the fire with only my doll for company. Human beings must love something and I loved my doll.

- **fainted:** lost consciousness
- **haunted by his ghost:** his ghost often appeared there

Love

Jane says: 'Human beings must love something.'
Do you agree?
Who and what do you love?

Only Bessie was nice to me and I preferred her to anyone else at Gateshead Hall. It was Bessie who, on the fifteenth of January, came running upstairs to find me in the nursery.

'They want to see you in the breakfast room,' she told me in a great hurry. She pushed me to the top of the stairs and went back into the nursery.

I slowly went down the stairs and entered the room. My aunt was sitting by the fire. A tall man in black stood beside her.

'This is the little girl that I wrote to you about,' said Mrs Reed.

The man turned his head towards me and looked at me for a long time.

'Your name, little girl?' he asked.

'Jane Eyre, sir,' I replied.

'Well, Jane Eyre, and are you a good child?'

Mrs Reed answered for me, 'The less said about that the better, Mr Brocklehurst.'

'Oh dear,' was his reply. 'I don't like naughty children. Do you know where wicked people go after they die?'

'They go to hell,' I answered.

'Do you say your prayers night and morning?' continued Mr Brocklehurst.

'Yes, sir.'

'Do you read your Bible?'

'Sometimes.'

'And the Psalms•? I hope you like them?'

'No, sir.'

'No? How shocking! That proves you have a wicked heart. You must pray and ask God to change it.'

'Mr Brocklehurst,' interrupted Mrs Reed. 'I hope you can accept this girl at Lowood School. She is deceitful• and a liar• and she must learn to be humble•. I would like to send her immediately. She will stay full-time and spend all the holidays there too.'

'Of course, madam,' said Mr Brocklehurst. 'Your decisions are wise. We will teach Miss Eyre humility• and obedience•. Our girls are all humble and obedient. We have great success at Lowood School.'

- **deceitful:** that hides the truth
- **humble:** not believing that you are important
- **humility:** being able to recognise your own bad qualities
- **liar:** someone who tells lies
- **obedience:** doing as you are told to do
- **Psalms:** sacred/holy songs and poems

Mr Brocklehurst left and I was alone with Mrs Reed. She started sewing•. Neither of us said anything. I was feeling angry with her. She said I was deceitful and a liar but I wasn't. I tried hard to be good but nothing I did was good enough for my aunt. She wanted me to suffer.

After a while she looked up from her sewing.

'Go back to the nursery,' she said.

I got up and went to the door, stopped and came back again. I had to tell her. I took a deep breath.

'I am not deceitful,' I said. 'And I'm not a liar. I don't say I love you, because I don't. I hate you more than anyone in the world, except John Reed. Your daughter Georgiana tells lies, but I don't.'

Mrs Reed looked at me.

'I will never call you aunt again,' I continued. 'I will tell people how you have treated me, how cruel you have been to me.'

'How dare you• say that, Jane Eyre!'

'How dare I, Mrs Reed? How dare I? Because it is the truth. You think I have no feelings and that I can survive without love or kindness. But I can't, and you have no pity•. You locked me in the red room because your wicked boy hit me. I'll tell anybody who asks me. I'll tell them the truth. People think you are a good woman but you are bad and mean. You are deceitful!'

- **how dare you:** used to express anger about something someone has done or said
- **pity:** feeling of sympathy and understanding
- **sewing:** 

2 Lowood School

2 A few days later Bessie woke me early. I had to leave Gateshead Hall that morning. Only Bessie accompanied me to the coach•. Mrs Reed didn't want to see me.

'Goodbye!' I cried as we passed through the hall and went out the front door. I was happy to leave. I wanted to start my new life.

Bessie hugged and kissed me.

'Take care of her,' she said to the guard as he helped me get into the coach.

It was fifty miles to Lowood. The coach journey was long and I eventually fell asleep.

I woke up when the coach stopped. It was now evening. A person like a servant was standing by the door of the coach.

'Is there a little girl called Jane Eyre here?' she asked.

'Yes,' I answered.

The guard lifted me up and put me down on the ground next to my trunk•. Then the coach drove away.

I looked around. Rain, wind and darkness filled the air. The servant girl and I went through a door of a big house.

A tall, important-looking lady met me in the hall. Behind her there was another lady.

• **coach:** carriage pulled by horses

• **trunk:** large strong box used for storing clothes or possessions (see image)

Miss Miller then took me away. The house was very large and she led me through lots of different rooms. I could hear the hum• of voices in the distance. Finally, we entered a long room. Girls of all ages were sitting on wooden benches• on each side of long tables. The youngest were about nine or ten and the oldest were twenty. All of them were dressed in the same brown wool dresses and white pinafores•. They were studying their books. The hum of voices was the girls repeating their lessons over and over to themselves. The number of girls sitting at the tables seemed infinite. I later learnt there were eighty girls at Lowood School.

Miss Miller told me to sit on a bench near the door. She then walked to the top of the long room.

'Monitors•! Collect the books and put them away!' she cried out loudly.

Four tall girls collected the books from the girls at the tables.

'Monitors, fetch the supper• trays•!' Miss Miller cried out.

The tall girls handed out portions of something from the trays. I couldn't eat because I was too excited and tired.

When the meal was over, Miss Miller read prayers. Then all the girls went upstairs to another very long room full of beds. Two girls got into each bed. That night I slept with Miss Miller. I fell asleep immediately. I was too tired even to dream.

- **bench:** 
- **hum:** continuous low sound
- **monitors:** children in school who have special jobs to do
- **pinafore:** 
- **supper:** dinner
- **tray:** 

School

What are Jane's first impressions of this school?

How is this school different from your school?

Discuss with a partner.

A loud bell rang the next morning to wake us up. It was still dark. It was very cold so I got dressed quickly. The bell rang again and we all went down to the schoolroom.

Miss Miller read prayers and then called out, 'Form classes!'

For more than an hour we read the Bible in our different classes. After that we marched into another room for breakfast. I was very hungry but the smell of the food in front of us was terrible.

'Disgusting! The porridge• is burnt again!' whispered• a girl.

'Silence!' shouted one of the teachers.

I quickly started eating but I stopped after one mouthful•. It really was too disgusting to eat. I looked around me. Spoons moved slowly. I saw each girl taste the porridge and try to swallow it but then most of them stopped eating too. When the bell rang at the end of breakfast, everyone was still hungry. I saw one of the teachers taste the porridge.

'It's disgusting! How shameful•!' she whispered to another teacher.

We went back to the schoolroom and formed our classes again. Before starting our lessons, everybody stood up. The tall important-looking lady from the night before entered the room. I later learnt her name was Miss Temple and she was the superintendent• of Lowood School. She taught the older girls.

When the clock struck twelve the superintendent stood up.

'This morning you couldn't eat your breakfast,' she said. 'You must all be hungry. I have ordered a lunch of bread and cheese for you all.'

The teachers looked at her in surprise.

'I'll take responsibility,' she added and then she left the room.

- **mouthful:** amount of food which fills your mouth
- **porridge:** thick soft food often eaten for breakfast

- **shameful:** that deserves to be criticised
- **superintendent:** person responsible for most things in a school
- **whispered:** said in a quiet voice

We ate our bread and cheese happily and then went out into the garden. The stronger girls ran around and played games but the pale, thin ones stood together trying to keep warm. Some of them had a bad cough•.

I stood on my own and no one spoke to me. But I wasn't lonely or sad. Being alone was normal for me. I looked up at the school building and read the inscription on a stone sign.

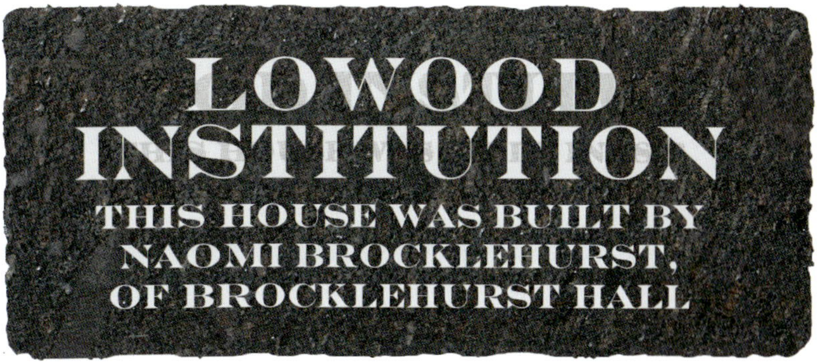

I was thinking about the word 'institution' when I heard someone coughing behind me. I turned and saw a girl sitting on a stone bench. She was reading a book.

'Is your book interesting?' I asked her.

'I like it,' she answered, looking at me carefully.

'Can you tell me what the word "institution" means?' I asked.

'It means this school is partly a charity school•,' she replied. 'We are all charity children. I suppose you are an orphan like the rest of us?' 'Yes,' I said.

- **charity school:** school helped by people giving money
- **cough:** sound that coughing (forcing air out of your lungs through your throat) makes

'And who was Naomi Brocklehurst?' I asked, wanting to know more.

'The lady who built the new part of this house. She is dead and her son owns Lowood now.'

'Then this house doesn't belong to that tall lady – the one who ordered the bread and cheese?'

'To Miss Temple? Oh, no, unfortunately! She works for Mr Brocklehurst.'

Mr Brocklehurst

What do you remember about Mr Brocklehurst?

Go back to page 24 and check.

'Does he live here?' I asked.

'No,' she said. 'He lives in a big house two miles away with his family. He is a clergyman•.'

'Do you like the teachers here?'

'They're alright.'

'How long have you been here?'

'Two years. But you ask too many questions,' she said to me. 'I want to read my book.'

Just at that moment the dinner bell rang and we had to go in.

• **clergyman:** priest in the Christian Church

3 Helen Burns

I soon learnt the name of my new friend because one of the teachers continually criticised her.

'Burns,' she said (the teachers called us by our surnames). 'Sit up straight!' Or: 'Burns, don't look at me like that!'

One day, as a punishment•, she had to stand in the middle of the schoolroom so that everybody could look at her.

When the girls in her class were tested, Burns knew all the answers. She knew more than all the other girls but the teacher never praised her•.

'Why are your nails so dirty, Burns?' was all she said to her.

I couldn't understand why the teacher punished her. She didn't do anything wrong. And every time she was punished or told off•, she never got angry. The teacher often criticised her but she never reacted. She kept her usual calm, humble expression even when that teacher hit her with the stick•. I saw her cry only once.

In the evenings we were allowed to rest for a whole hour. One evening I found Burns sitting by the fire. She was reading the same book as before. I went and sat down next to her.

'What's your first name, Burns?' I asked her.

'Helen,' she replied.

'Would you like to leave Lowood?'

'No! Why? I was sent here to get an education.'

'But that teacher is so cruel to you!'

'Cruel? Not at all! She's strict•. I have faults• and she corrects them.'

- **faults:** negative aspects of a person's character
- **praised her:** told her she was good
- **punishment:** when someone is treated badly after they do something wrong.
- **stick:** 
- **strict:** punishes if she is not obeyed
- **told off:** critcize someone for doing something wrong

'But she hit you,' I cried. 'And you aren't a bad girl. You're very clever. How can you not be angry with her? If she hits me, I won't be able to keep quiet.'

'You must,' Helen replied. 'Mr Brocklehurst expels• pupils• if they don't obey the rules. We must obey and not cause problems for other people. The Bible teaches us to love our enemies and to be good to them even when they hurt us.'

I couldn't believe it. How could Helen be so forgiving? She didn't do anything wrong but the teacher hit her. She was a cruel, bad-tempered• woman.

'Does Miss Temple treat you badly too?' I asked.

'Oh, no,' Helen replied. 'Miss Temple is good. But when I make mistakes she tells me. It's bad to make mistakes and I must learn to be a better person. You're still young and you'll learn this.'

'But Helen,' I began. 'If someone is unkind to me or punishes me unjustly•, I dislike them. It's natural. Like it's natural to love someone when they are kind to you and accept punishment when you deserve it.'

I could see that Helen didn't agree with me. We didn't talk any more that evening.

Points of view

Who do you agree with, Helen or Jane?

Why? Discuss with a partner.

- **bad-tempered:** who gets angry easily
- **expels:** forces to leave the school
- **pupils:** young students
- **unjustly:** without good reason

e-ZONE ONLINE ACTIVITIES Chapters 1-3

4 Mr Brocklehurst

My first winter at Lowood was long and hard. It often snowed and it was very cold. Our clothes didn't keep us warm. We were given very little food and were constantly cold and hungry.

But the worst thing that happened to me that winter was Mr Brocklehurst's first visit to Lowood.

One afternoon soon after my arrival at Lowood, a tall black figure entered the schoolroom. I recognized Mr Brocklehurst immediately. Everybody stopped writing on their slates• and stood up. Even the teachers stood up. I felt very afraid. Mr Brocklehurst had false information about me from Mrs Reed. I was sure he wanted to tell everyone I was a liar.

He talked to Miss Temple about the school. He complained about a lot of things. The girls had too much to eat, their clothes were washed too often, some of the girls' hair wasn't completely straight and even that some of the girls were growing too tall. Miss Temple listened to these absurd complaints and tried not to show her anger.

All this time I was hiding my face behind my slate because I didn't want Mr Brocklehurst to see me. But then to my horror I dropped it. It fell to the floor and broke into pieces. Everybody turned to look at me.

'Ah, the new girl!' said Mr Brocklehurst. 'I have something to say about her. Come here girl.'

The girls next to me pushed me forward. Two monitors lifted me onto a stool•. The stool was in the middle of the room and everybody was looking at me.

• **slate:** 

• **stool:** 

'Girls! Teachers!' said Mr Brocklehurst. 'Can you all see this girl? She is young and healthy. But I must warn you about her. She is evil and she is a liar! I learnt this from her benefactor•, Mrs Reed. That good lady treated her well but this girl was deceitful and dishonest. Mrs Reed sent this girl here to learn to be good and honest. Teachers! You must watch her and punish her when she is naughty. Girls! You must not play with her or speak to her. Perhaps we'll manage to save her soul. Now she will stay on the stool for another half hour.'

With these words Mr Brocklehurst left the room.

My punishment was so unjust. I felt furious• and humiliated•. My face was burning and it was difficult for me to breathe. I couldn't look at anyone.

But then someone walked past me. It was Helen Burns. When she passed again she looked up at me and smiled. What a smile! I remember it now. Her smile gave me strength and I stood on my stool with my head up high.

Humiliation

Why is Jane's punishment unjust?

Have you ever felt humiliated?

Discuss with a partner.

The clock struck five. My half hour was over so I got off the stool and went to the corner of the now empty room. I started to cry. I was trying so hard to be good at Lowood and to make a new start. I was good at my schoolwork and the teachers liked me. But now everybody thought I was a liar. This made me cry even harder.

- **benefactor:** someone who gives money to help an organisation, society or person
- **furious:** very angry
- **humiliated:** treated without respect

Then Helen arrived. She brought me some coffee and bread from the dining room but I didn't want to eat or drink anything. Helen sat down next to me while I continued to cry.

I spoke first.

'Helen, why do you stay with me? Everybody thinks I am a liar and hates me.'

'They don't hate you. They pity you,' Helen replied. 'No one likes Mr Brocklehurst. They'll quickly forget his words if you continue to be a good girl. You'll see. Their coldness will soon change to kindness.'

I didn't say anything. Helen made me feel calm. I put my head on her shoulder and my arms around her. I was still holding her when a figure approached. It was Miss Temple.

'I came to find you, Jane Eyre,' she said. 'I want to talk to you. Helen Burns, you can come too.'

We followed her to her room and she told us to sit down.

'Have you finished crying?' Miss Temple asked me, looking at my face.

'No,' I replied.

'Why not?'

'Because I have been wrongly accused•. And you, ma'am•, and everybody else, will now think I'm wicked.'

'Well, Jane,' Miss Temple said kindly. 'I'd like to hear what you have to say. Tell me your story, but I want the truth.'

So I told Miss Temple my story. I tried to include all the facts and the names of the people involved. I also included my own faults and tried hard not to show my feelings of hate.

Miss Temple looked at me for a few minutes in silence. Then she said, 'I know Mr Lloyd, the doctor you talked about. I will write to him. If he tells me the same things as you have told me, you will be publicly cleared• of every accusation. For me, Jane, you are clear now.'

With these kind words Miss Temple kissed me and then turned to Helen.

'How is your cough tonight, Helen?'

'It is a little better,' Helen replied.

Miss Temple then called for tea and toast. That evening we feasted• on food, warmth, kindness and affection.

About a week later, Miss Temple received an answer from Mr Lloyd. He said that I was telling the truth. That day Miss Temple announced to everyone that Jane Eyre wasn't guilty• of Mr Brocklehurst's accusations. The teachers kissed me and my companions all smiled at me. I was so happy.

- **feasted:** ate lots and well
- **ma'am:** polite title for a woman (madam)
- **publicly cleared:** shown to be innocent in public
- **wasn't guilty:** was innocent
- **wrongly accused:** unjustly considered guilty

5 Illness

MP3

My name now cleared, I worked very hard at my lessons. I was moved to a higher class and I started to learn French and drawing.

Spring came and brought warmer weather but it also brought typhus•. Many girls caught the fever• and in May part of Lowood was transformed into a hospital.

Little food and bad coughs and colds made pupils weak•. Forty-five of the eighty girls at the school were ill. Classes were less frequent and rules were relaxed because the teachers were all busy with the patients. Some girls were sent home either to escape the fever or to die. Some died at the school.

Lowood became an even sadder place and was filled with fear. The only way to escape was to go out into the garden. There we could enjoy the warm spring weather, the flowers and walks in the woods.

I remained healthy but my dear friend Helen Burns didn't. She was taken to a room upstairs and I wasn't allowed to see her. I often thought about her and asked the teachers how she was. On one occasion I was given the answer, 'She won't be with us for much longer.'

I knew this meant death and not a journey back to her home. I was determined to see her once more before she died.

A nurse told me that she was in Miss Temple's room so I went to find her. She was lying in bed behind a curtain.

'Helen,' I whispered softly. 'Are you awake?'

'Is that you, Jane?' she asked in her sweet voice.

I got on her bed and kissed her. Her body was thin and cold.

- **fever:** very high body temperature
- **typhus:** infectious disease
- **weak:** not strong

'I've come to see you, Helen.'

'You came to say goodbye. I think you are just in time.'

'Where are you going, Helen? Are you going home?'

'Yes. To my last home.'

'No, no, Helen!' I cried.

'Stay with me, Jane. Don't leave me!' Helen said. 'I am very happy. I am going to God. He loves me. Hold me, Jane.'

'Good night, Helen. I won't leave you. I'll stay with you.'

She kissed me and I kissed her and we both fell asleep.

That night Helen died in my arms.

Many girls died of the fever – so many that people began to ask questions. They soon learnt about the awful• conditions in the school and changes had to be made. Mr Brocklehurst no longer had so much control. A committee• made the decisions. These changes were all good for us pupils. There was more comfort, more compassion, and, more importantly, more food. The school started slowly to become a really useful institution.

I spent another eight years at Lowood: six as a pupil and two as a teacher. I studied and worked hard and learnt a lot in this time. Then Miss Temple, who was a mother, teacher and later a companion to me, married and left the school. I missed her a lot and I began to think it was time for me to leave Lowood too.

I thought long and hard about what to do. In the end I decided to put an advertisement in the newspaper.

A young lady is looking for a job as a governess in a private family with children under fourteen years of age. She is qualified to teach all general subjects including French, drawing and music.

A few days later I received a reply.

A private family requires a governess for a little girl under ten years of age. The salary• is thirty pounds a year. Please send references• and details to Mrs Fairfax, Thornfield, near Millcote.

- **awful:** terrible
- **committee:** small group of chosen people who make decisions
- **references:** letters describing a person's qualities and character
- **salary:** money paid for a job

I read the letter carefully. I hoped so much that the job and the family were respectable. I was alone in the world and had no one to give me advice.

I told the superintendent about the job, adding that the salary was good. I also asked her to tell Mr Brocklehurst and the committee. I wanted to ask them for references.

Mr Brocklehurst said that I had to ask Mrs Reed for permission because she was my legal guardian. So I wrote to her. I received a letter back saying, I could do what I wanted. The committee eventually gave me permission to leave and the necessary references.

Now I was all ready to become a governess at Thornfield Hall!

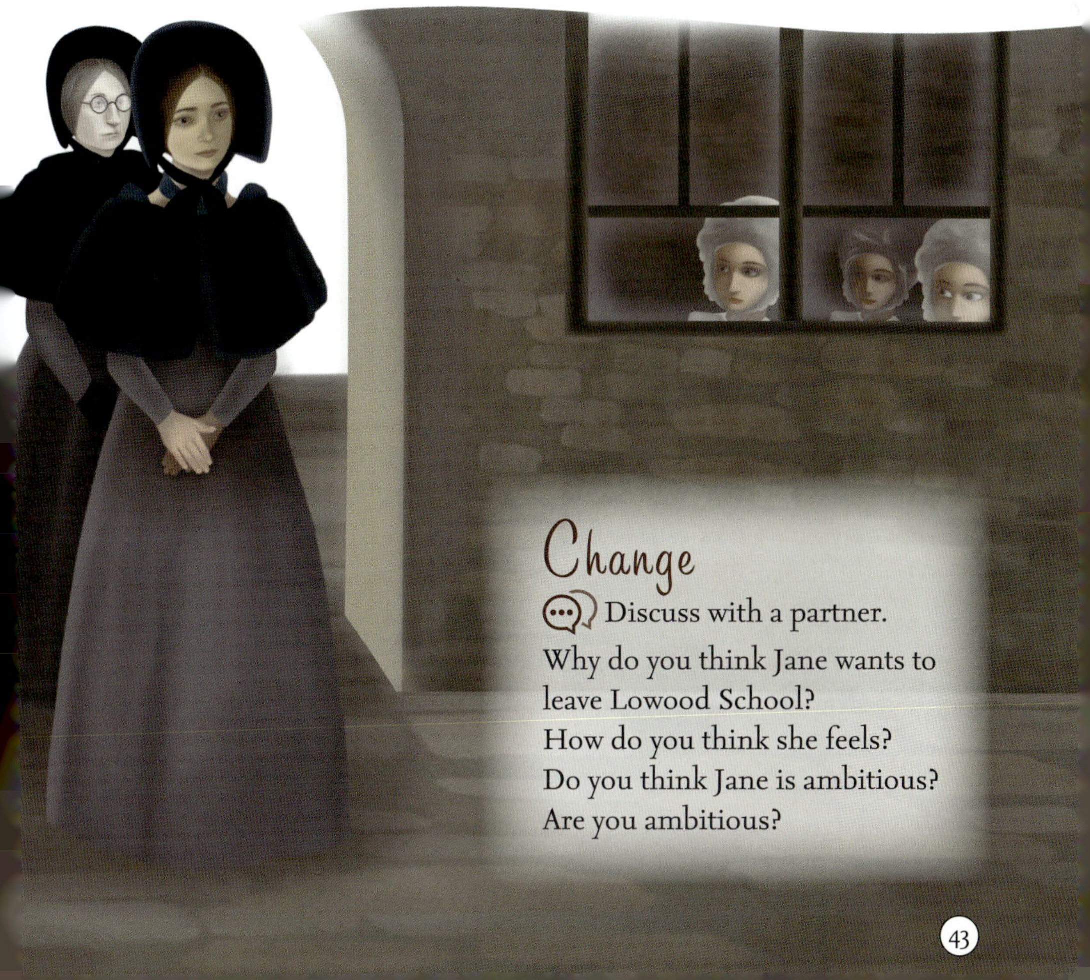

Change

Discuss with a partner.

Why do you think Jane wants to leave Lowood School?

How do you think she feels?

Do you think Jane is ambitious?

Are you ambitious?

6 Thornfield Hall

It took sixteen hours to get to Millcote so I had lots of time to think about my new employer Mrs Fairfax. I hoped she wasn't another Mrs Reed. When I arrived, a carriage• was waiting to take me to Thornfield Hall.

Two hours later it stopped in front of a large, long house. A girl opened the door and I went inside.

She took me to a small comfortable room with a cheerful fire. A little old lady was sitting next to it. She was knitting•.

'How do you do, my dear?' she said, getting up to meet me. 'You've had a long journey. Come to the fire. You must be cold.'

'Mrs Fairfax?' I asked.

'Yes. Please sit down.'

She helped me take off my bonnet• and shawl• and told the girl to take them to my room.

'Then bring Miss Eyre something to eat,' she said.

'She's treating me like a visitor,' I thought. I wasn't expecting such kindness from an employer.

'Will I have the pleasure of seeing Miss Fairfax tonight?' I asked.

'Miss Fairfax? Oh, you mean Miss Varens! Adela Varens is the name of your pupil.'

'Oh! Then she isn't your daughter?'

'No, I have no family. I'm glad that you've come. Thornfield can be lonely in the winter. Before I only had the servants to talk to. But now Adela, her nurse and you are here, so we'll all have a happy time together.'

Mrs Fairfax continued to talk while I ate. I liked her more and more.

- **bonnet:** 
- **carriage:** (here) vehicle with four wheels pulled by horses
- **knitting:** 
- **shawl:** 

That night I slept very well. Mrs Fairfax was kind and my room was safe and warm.

When I woke up the next morning it was already light. The room looked lovely in the sunlight. It was very different from the one I had at Lowood.

'I'm going to like working here,' I thought happily.

I got dressed and went to explore. Downstairs the front door was open so I went out into the garden. It was a lovely autumn day and I could see trees and hills in the distance. As I was enjoying the view and the fresh air, Mrs Fairfax appeared at the door.

'How do you like Thornfield?' she asked. I told her I liked it very much.

'Yes,' she said, 'it's a pretty place. But Mr Rochester needs to spend more time here.'

'Mr Rochester!' I exclaimed. 'Who's he?'

'The owner of Thornfield,' she replied. 'Didn't you know?'

'I thought that Thornfield belonged to you•.'

'To me? My dear child! What an idea! I'm only the housekeeper•.'

Mr Rochester

What do you think Mr Rochester will be like?
Make a list of what we know about him so far.
Add to your list as you continue reading.

- **belonged to you:** (here) was your house
- **housekeeper:** servant who looks after someone's house

'And the little girl – my pupil?'

'She's Mr Rochester's ward•. He asked me to find a governess for her. Look! Here she is with her nurse.'

A pretty little girl with long curly hair ran towards us.

'Good morning, Miss Adela,' said Mrs Fairfax. 'Say hello to Miss Eyre. She's going to teach you and make you a clever lady.'

'Bonjour,' said Adela. She turned to her nurse, who was standing behind her, and asked her a question in French.

'Does she speak English?' I asked Mrs Fairfax.

'A little, but Sophie, her nurse, doesn't speak any at all,' said Mrs Fairfax.

I was glad my French was good and Adela was very happy to discover I spoke her language.

'You speak French as well as Mr Rochester does,' she exclaimed.

She told me that after her mother died, Mr Rochester brought her and Sophie from France to England in a great ship. Then they came to live at Thornfield. Now Mr Rochester was no longer here and he never came to see her.

After breakfast, Adela and I went to the library. This was our schoolroom. There were books, a globe, a piano and an easel• for painting.

We had lessons until noon•, then I sent Adela back to Sophie. I decided to spend the afternoon doing some drawings for Adela's lessons the next day so I went upstairs to get some paper and pencils.

• **easel:** 

• **noon:** twelve o'clock in the middle of the day

• **ward:** (here) child legally under Mr Rochester's protection

When I was on the stairs, Mrs Fairfax called to me from a room that she was cleaning.

'Your morning school hours are over now, I suppose.'

I went back down to speak to her. The room was very grand. It had purple chairs and curtains and there was a Turkish carpet on the floor.

'What a beautiful room!' I exclaimed as I looked round. 'And how tidy you keep it.'

'Yes,' Mrs Fairfax replied. 'Mr Rochester's visits here are rare. But they are always sudden and unexpected. He often brings visitors. I like to have everything ready for him when he comes.'

'What's Mr Rochester like?' I asked.

'He's a gentleman, a good master and respected by everyone. He's very clever but perhaps he's a little strange.'

'In what way, strange?'

'I don't know, it isn't easy to describe. It's difficult to understand if he's happy or not.'

Then Mrs Fairfax showed me all the other rooms in the house – downstairs and upstairs. Finally, she took me out through the attic and onto the roof.

'The view is wonderful from here,' she said.

The garden and the countryside looked lovely in the bright autumn light and when we came in again, the attic seemed very, very dark. Suddenly I heard a strange noise. It was a low laugh. I stopped and listened. Then I heard it again.

'Did you hear that laugh?' I asked Mrs Fairfax. 'Who was it?'

'One of the servants, I expect,' she answered. 'Perhaps it was Grace Poole.'

I heard the noise again.

'Grace!' exclaimed Mrs Fairfax.

The door of one of the attic rooms opened and a woman came out. She was about forty years old and she had red hair and a plain face.

'There's too much noise, Grace,' said Mrs Fairfax. 'Remember your orders!'

The woman nodded silently and went in.

'Grace works here. She does the sewing and other jobs,' Mrs Fairfax told me. 'Now, tell me, how was your pupil, Miss Adela, this morning?'

Grace Poole was immediately forgotten and our conversation about Adela continued until we got downstairs.

Guess

Why does Grace Poole have to work in the attic?
What are the orders that she must remember?

7 Mr Rochester

5 I was happy at Thornfield Hall. Mrs Fairfax was a kind, calm, sensible person. My pupil was a lively, affectionate child and tried hard to please me. She was difficult to teach at first because she was spoilt• but she soon became obedient and made good progress in her lessons.

I had no reason to complain about my life at Thornfield Hall but I was often bored. My only relief• was to walk – sometimes around the garden, sometimes up and down the corridor on the third floor, and other times on the roof.

When I was on the third floor, I often heard Grace Poole laughing. There were days when she was very quiet but there were other days when she laughed loudly. Sometimes when I saw her, I spoke to her but she never wanted to talk and went back to her room in the attic.

October, November and December passed. In January, Adela caught a cold and wasn't well enough to do her lessons. Having the afternoon free, I offered to walk to Hay, a village two miles away, to post a letter for Mrs Fairfax. It was a very cold day so I walked fast to keep warm. I was nearly halfway there when the sound of a horse galloping at great speed broke the silence. I stopped and waited for it to pass. A moment later I heard a loud crash. I ran back to see what it was.

The horse and its rider were on the ground.

'Are you injured, sir?' I asked.

The man didn't reply so I asked again, 'Can I do anything?'

'Please, just move out of my way,' he answered.

- **complexion:** colour of the skin
- **relief:** reason to be happy
- **spoilt:** (here) was able to do what she wanted and so was selfish

He was a man of about thirty-five with black hair and a dark complexion• – not very handsome. I didn't feel afraid or shy. In fact his angry expression made me like him so I didn't move away.

'I cannot think of leaving you, sir,' I said. 'It's late and you are alone. I must be sure that you are able to ride your horse before I go.'

He looked at me when I said this. It was the first time his eyes met mine.

'Why aren't you at home?' the man asked me. 'Where have you come from?'

'From Thornfield,' I answered. 'I'm going to Hay to post a letter.'

'Whose house is Thornfield?'

'Mr Rochester's.'

'Do you know Mr Rochester?'

'No, I've never seen him.'

'You aren't a servant at the hall, of course. You are...' He stopped. He looked at my clothes. He seemed puzzled about what I was so I helped him.

'I'm the governess.'

'Ah, the governess!' he repeated. 'Of course. The governess!' He tried to stand up but the pain in his leg was very bad.

'I don't want you to go and get help,' he said. 'But you can help me a little yourself, if you will be so kind.'

'Yes, sir.'

'Try to bring my horse to me.'

I tried to catch the horse but it was very excited and I wasn't able to take hold of it. The man waited and watched for some time and then he laughed.

'I see,' he said. 'If my horse won't come to me, I must go to my horse. Please come and help me.'

He put his hand on my shoulder and we slowly walked to his horse. He caught it easily and jumped on it despite the pain in his ankle. He was obviously a good horseman.

The horseman

Who do you think this man is?

'Thank you,' he said. 'Now go quickly to Hay and post your letter. Then hurry home as fast as you can.'

He rode away with his dog running after him.

I posted my letter in Hay and walked back to Thornfield. It was getting dark now. I stopped for a few minutes at the place where I met and helped the traveller. The incident was unimportant but it gave me something to think about. A new face, a new memory. I didn't want to go back to Thornfield straight away. I didn't want to lose that memory and return to my safe but boring life there.

It was completely dark when I eventually opened the door of Thornfield Hall and went in. I could hear voices in the dining room. One of them was Adela's. I went to Mrs Fairfax's room. A dog, just like the traveller's dog, was sitting in front of the fire. I called a servant to ask for information.

'Whose dog is this?'

'He came with the master, Mr Rochester. He has just arrived and is with the others in the dining room. John has gone to get the doctor because the master had an accident. His horse fell and he hurt his ankle.'

'I see,' I said. I took a candle and I went upstairs to change my dress before dinner.

I didn't see Mr Rochester again that night. He followed the doctor's orders and went to bed early.

The next day there was a lot of movement and life in the house. Adela was very excited too.

'Mr Rochester has a present for me,' she told me. 'It's in his trunk.'

Late in the afternoon when the house was quieter, Mrs Fairfax came to my room.

'Mr Rochester would like you and Adela to have tea with him in the drawing room later,' she said. 'You must change your dress. I'll help you.'

'Is it really necessary?' I asked.

'Yes,' she replied 'When Mr Rochester is at Thornfield, I always do.'

Adela was already sitting at Mr Rochester's feet by the fire. He didn't look up to greet us as we entered the room so we sat down quietly and waited. Mrs Fairfax tried to make conversation but Mr Rochester neither spoke nor moved. When the tea tray was brought in, Adela and I moved to the table but he stayed on his sofa.

'Please take Mr Rochester his tea,' Mrs Fairfax said, giving me his cup.

'Did you bring Miss Eyre a present too?' asked Adela as Mr Rochester took the teacup from my hand.

'A present?' said Mr Rochester, turning to look at me for the first time. 'Did you expect a present, Miss Eyre?'

'No, sir,' I replied. 'You don't know me and I've done nothing to deserve one.'

'That isn't true,' Mr Rochester replied. 'You have done good work with Adela. She has made a lot of progress.'

'Sir,' I said. 'That is my present. Praise of her pupils' progress is the best thing you can give a teacher.'

'Humph!' said Mr Rochester and he drank his tea in silence.

'Come nearer the fire!' he said when tea was over.

He began asking me questions about Lowood and my family situation. Then he ordered me to play a tune on the piano and show him some of my drawings. He was obviously trying to test me. He wanted to provoke me and see how I reacted. But I was strong and able to play his game. So, I replied to his questions politely using the same tone of voice as he used with me.

At last, tired of our company, he told us all to go to bed.

Provocation

Are you easily provoked?
How do you react when people provoke you?

'I think Mr Rochester is strange and complicated,' I said later to Mrs Fairfax.

'Maybe,' she replied. 'But we must forgive him for that. It's partly his nature but also because he has many problems.'

'What kind of problems?' I asked.

'Family problems. Many are linked to this house. I think that's why he never stays at Thornfield for long periods of time.'

I wanted to know more but it was clear from Mrs Fairfax's expression that she didn't want to talk any more about him.

e-ZONE ONLINE ACTIVITIES Chapters 4-7

8 The Fire

For the next few days I saw little of Mr Rochester. He was always busy or out on his horse.

One evening, however, he sent for Adela and I after dinner. He was in a good mood• and gave Adela the present she was waiting for.

'Now go away and open it,' he said. 'And don't bother me any more with your chatter•.'

Then he turned to me and said, 'Come and sit over here, Miss Eyre. I want to be able to see you without having to change my position in this comfortable chair.'

He sat looking into the fire for a couple of minutes and I observed him for the same amount of time. He had large dark eyes. They were fine eyes, full of great feeling.

'You're examining me, Miss Eyre,' he said, looking at me. 'Do you think I'm handsome?'

'No, sir,' I replied without thinking.

'Ha, ha,' he laughed. 'You're a very unusual girl, Miss Eyre. You look very serious and quiet but when you have to answer questions you're surprisingly frank• and honest.'

I was embarrassed and tried to apologise. But he liked my honesty. That evening we talked for a long time. I learnt that he didn't have a very good opinion of himself because of a mistake he made in his past. He regretted it• now and wanted to be a better person. He also wanted to find happiness.

- **don't bother...chatter:** leave me in peace
- **frank:** that says what he thinks
- **in a good mood:** happy
- **regretted it:** was sorry he did it

One afternoon, a short time after our long talk, I was outside with Adela when Mr Rochester suddenly appeared. Adela starting playing with his dog so Mr Rochester and I walked around the garden. He talked about his past and about Adela.

'She was the daughter of a Parisian dancer named Celine Varens,' he said. 'I was once in love with Celine but she deceived me and ran away to Italy with another admirer. She left her daughter, Adela, in Paris. She said I was the child's father but I know I'm not. I don't know who is. The poor little girl has no one else and I want to help her. I don't know why I'm telling you all this. I hope you won't leave now you know the story. Are you shocked?'

'No,' I replied. 'I will love Adela even more now I know.'

And so Mr Rochester and I gradually became friends. He was less moody• and often wanted to talk. Our conversations made me happy and filled a gap• in my life. I felt alive when I was with him. He was trying to be a better person but there was always the presence of an unknown sadness inside him that was still a mystery to me.

Sadness

What kind of events in life make people very sad?
What could be the cause of the unknown sadness that Mr Rochester has inside him?

- **flood:** large amount of water covering a place that is usually dry
- **gap:** empty space
- **moody:** (here) unfriendly
- **jug:**

- **washbasin:**

That night I lay in bed and thought about Mr Rochester. 'Will he leave Thornfield soon?' I wondered. 'Mrs Fairfax says he never stays here very long. He's been here for eight weeks now. The house will be a sad place if he goes.'

Then suddenly I heard a strange sound. It seemed to be above me. I sat up; my heart was beating fast. A clock struck two. Someone or something passed the door of my room.

'Who's there?' I called.

There was no answer. I began to feel frightened. Then I heard the low deep laugh. Was it Grace Poole? I had to find out. I got up and went out into the corridor. I was surprised to see a candle burning there. And then I noticed smoke and the smell of burning.

The smoke was coming from Mr Rochester's bedroom. The door was open so I went inside. The curtains around his bed were on fire!

'Wake up! Wake up!' I shouted, but he didn't move.

I ran to the washbasin•, picked up the water jug• and threw the water on the flames. Then I threw the water from a vase onto Mr Rochester's face and finally he woke up.

'Is there a flood•?' he cried finding himself lying in a pool of water.

'No, sir,' I answered. 'But there was a fire.'

'What happened?' he asked, getting out of his wet bed. He listened with a very serious look on his face while I told him. Then he said, 'I must go to the attic. Stay here until I return. Don't move or call anyone.'

When he came back, he looked pale and depressed.

'It's just as I thought,' he said.

'What is, sir?' I asked.

'You said that you heard a laugh. Have you heard that laugh before?'

'Yes, sir. The woman who sews – Grace Poole. She laughs like that. She's a strange person.'

'Exactly. Grace Poole – you are right. She is, as you say, strange – very. Jane, only you and I know about this incident. Do you understand me? Please say nothing to the servants. I'll talk to them about it tomorrow. Now we must sleep.'

'Yes, sir. Good night, then, sir,' I said, turning to leave.

'Where are you going, Jane?' Rochester exclaimed.

'You told me to go, sir.'

'But you must say goodbye properly. You have just saved my life! At least shake hands with me.'

He held out his hand. I gave him mine. He took it and held it in both his hands, looking at me with a strange fire in his eyes.

'I knew you were a special person as soon as I saw you. You're good for me, Jane.'

'I'm glad I was awake,' I said and went back to my room but I couldn't sleep.

9 Blanche Ingram

MP3 I both wanted and was afraid to see Mr Rochester after my sleepless night. But I didn't meet him the following day. When I went past his room later I found Grace Poole sewing new curtains for his bed. I couldn't believe it and I felt I had to test her.

'Good morning, Grace,' I said. 'What a strange incident! Did Mr Rochester really not wake anybody up? And didn't anyone hear him putting out the fire?'

She raised her eyes to me and said, 'Perhaps you heard a noise, Miss?'

'I did,' I said quietly. 'I heard a strange laugh.'

She looked at me again and said, 'Then I think you should lock your door carefully every night.'

At that moment a servant entered the room. She told me that Mrs Fairfax was waiting for me so I had to leave Grace Poole.

For the rest of the day I thought about this mystery. Why didn't Mr Rochester punish Grace Poole for what she did? I wanted to see him to ask him. I asked Mrs Fairfax where he was.

'Mr Rochester has gone to visit friends on the other side of Millcote,' she told me. 'They're having a big party.'

'Will he come back tonight?' I asked.

'Oh, no. I think he'll stay there for a week or more. He's popular at their parties, especially with the ladies.'

'Which ladies?' I asked.

'Most of them,' she replied. 'But in particular with Blanche Ingram. She's the most beautiful of all. I saw her when she came here for a Christmas ball.'

'What's she like?'

• **glossiest:** that shine the most

Jane

Why is Jane surprised at Mr Rochester?
Why does she ask about Blanche Ingram?
What do you think Jane feels for Mr Rochester?

'Tall with a good figure, lovely olive skin and eyes like jewels. And she has wonderful hair! Dark with the glossiest• curls you ever saw. She can sing well, too. I even heard her sing with Mr Rochester.'

Alone in my room that night I forced myself to look in the mirror.

'Fool!' I told myself, looking at my reflection. 'You are a poor governess with a plain face. How can you think you are important to Mr Rochester? Think of Blanche Ingram and remember who you are.'

Two weeks went by and there was no news of Mr Rochester. I tried to forget my feelings for him. I worked hard with Adela and in my free time I sewed and drew. I wanted to be busy. I even thought about leaving Thornfield and getting another job.

Then a letter arrived. I waited anxiously while Mrs Fairfax read it.

'Does Mr Rochester say when he's coming home?' I asked, trying not to sound interested.

'Yes, he does,' she replied. 'He's arriving with a big party of guests in three days. We have to get the house ready for their arrival.'

There was lots to do. Even Adela and I were asked to help in the preparations.

One afternoon while we were working, I heard two of the servants talking about Grace Poole.

'At least she is well paid,' said one.

'Oh yes,' the other replied. 'She gets five times our salary. But she deserves it for the job she has to do.'

Then they noticed I was listening and quickly walked away.

So now I knew for sure that there was a mystery at Thornfield but I still didn't really know any more about it.

Salaries

Why do you think Grace Poole has such a good salary?
Do you think people should have different salaries for different jobs?
What kind of people have the highest/lowest salaries in your country?
Discuss with a partner.

The guests arrived – some in carriages, others on horseback. Adela and I watched them from an upstairs window. A beautiful lady was riding next to Mr Rochester. She matched Mrs Fairfax's description of Blanche Ingram.

The following evening Adela and I were called down to join the party. Adela was soon making friends with all the ladies while I sat alone in a corner observing the scene. Blanche Ingram was without doubt the most beautiful woman in the room, even if her expression was a little haughty•.

After coffee, she and Mr Rochester stood near the fireplace talking. I heard her invite him to sing while she played the piano. I listened to them for a while and then left through a side door.

I was on the stairs when Mr Rochester called me back.

'How are you, Jane?' he asked.

'I am very well, sir.'

'Why didn't you come and speak to me in the drawing room?'

'I didn't want to disturb you. You seemed busy, sir.'

'You look pale and a little depressed,' he said. 'What's wrong? Tell me.'

'Nothing – nothing, sir. I'm not depressed.'

'Well, tonight I excuse you. But while my visitors are here, I'd like you to come and join our party every evening. I insist. Now, good night, my…'

He stopped, bit his lip, turned round and walked away.

• **haughty:** arrogant and superior towards others

In the days that followed I watched Mr Rochester and Blanche Ingram. Although I loved Mr Rochester I wasn't jealous of Miss Ingram. She had no qualities to be jealous of. She was pretty and could play the piano and sing nicely but her mind was empty. Her conversation was learnt from books, nothing she said was original. She wasn't tender or sympathetic and she had no interest in Adela. It was clear, however, that Mr Rochester intended to marry her, perhaps for family reasons, perhaps political reasons, or perhaps because her position in society and connections were useful to him. But I knew that he didn't love her.

10 Secrets

MP3 One night, while the guests were still at Thornfield, a man arrived and asked to speak to Mr Rochester.

'My name is Mason and I've just arrived from the West Indies,' he said. He asked me to inform Mr Rochester of his arrival so I went to look for him and found him in the library.

'His name is Mason, sir, and he comes from the West Indies. From Spanish Town, in Jamaica, I think.'

On hearing the name Mr Rochester suddenly turned very pale. He grabbed my hand and seemed to stop breathing.

'Mason! The West Indies!' he said in a strange voice.

'Do you feel ill, sir?' I asked.

'I feel weak, Jane,' he said almost falling.

'Oh! Lean• on me, sir.'

'Jane, you offered me your shoulder once before. I'll have it again now.'

'Yes, sir. Here! Take my arm.'

He sat down and made me sit beside him. Holding my hand in both of his, he looked at me with worried eyes.

'My little friend!' he said. 'I'd like to be on a desert island with only you. I'd have no problems then.'

'Can I help you, sir? I'd do anything for you.'

'Bring him to me, Jane, and then leave us.'

'Yes, sir.'

I did this and much later, when I was in bed, I heard Mr Rochester show Mr Mason to his room. I hoped that was the end of Mr Rochester's troubles.

• **lean:** rest

In the middle of the night I was woken by a terrible scream. Then I heard a man calling for help. A little later Mr Rochester knocked on my door.

'Are you up and dressed, Jane?'

'Yes, sir.'

'Then come with me. Be as quiet as you can.'

I followed him up to the attic. I expected to see Grace Poole there and was surprised to see Mr Mason. He was alone. He was sitting on a chair and one of his arms was covered in blood.

'Clean his wound•,' Mr Rochester said to me. 'I'm going to get the doctor. Don't speak to this man while I'm away – not a word! And Richard, if you open your mouth and frighten this girl, you'll know all the force of my anger!'

He left and locked the door. I was scared but I followed his instructions and cleaned Mr Mason's wound in silence.

'What is this mystery?' I thought. 'First fire and now blood.'

I was glad when Mr Rochester came back with the doctor. He put a bandage• on the wound and then helped Mr Rochester take Mr Mason down the stairs. They put him into a carriage and he left just before the servants woke up.

It was getting light now and the spring air was fresh and clean. Mr Rochester suddenly picked a rose from a bush and gave it to me.

'Thank you again, Jane,' he said taking my hand and holding it tightly.

• **bandage:** 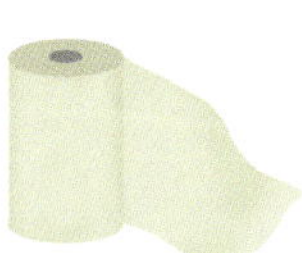

• **wound:** injury; cut in the skin

The following afternoon I received a message from Gateshead Hall. John Reed was dead and my aunt, Mrs Reed, was dying. She wanted to see me.

I went immediately to ask Mr Rochester for permission to leave. I found him playing billiards• with Miss Ingram.

When he saw me, he followed me out of the room.

'Well, Jane?' he said.

'Sir, please can I go away for a week or two?'

'To do what? To go where?'

I explained about my aunt. Mr Rochester didn't understand why I wanted to go but finally he gave me some of my wages• and made me promise to return.

'I'd like to say something else, sir,' I said. 'I believe you are planning to marry Miss Ingram. When you do, Adela should go to school. You won't need me any more so I'll look for a new job.'

I didn't want to be at Thornfield with Blanche Ingram as Mrs Rochester.

'Don't do that yet, Jane,' he said. And again he made me promise to return as soon as possible before eventually letting me go.

When I arrived at Gateshead Hall, Bessie met me and gave me tea. Everything in the house was the same and memories of my life there started to come back to me.

Later, Bessie took me to see Mrs Reed in her bedroom. I was determined to forget my feelings of bitterness• and hate towards this woman. I wanted very much to forgive all her wrongdoings•.

- **billiards:** 
- **bitterness:** intense bad feeling
- **wages:** salary
- **wrongdoings:** bad actions

I went up to her. Her face was still stern• and hard. She didn't respond when I touched or kissed her. I knew then that her feelings for me were the same as when I was a child. I was a bad girl in her mind and she had no intention of changing her opinion of me. This hurt me and then it made me angry, but I was determined not to let her upset• me.

My aunt wanted to tell me something but she waited until she was sure we were alone.

'Well, Jane Eyre,' she said. 'I have done two bad things to you. I regret them now and I don't want to die without telling you about them. The first thing – I promised my husband to bring you up as my own child and I broke that promise. The other – well, go to my jewellery box, open it, and take out the letter you'll see there.'

I did as she instructed and brought her the letter.

'Read it,' she said.

Madam,
Will you please send me the address of my niece, Jane Eyre, and tell me how she is? I would like to write and ask her to come and live with me in Madeira. I have a good job but I have never married and have no children. I'd like to adopt her• and then leave her everything I have when I die.
JOHN EYRE, Madeira.

The date on the letter was three years before.

- **adopt her:** legally become her father
- **stern:** serious; unfriendly
- **upset:** make sad

'Why didn't you tell me about this?' I asked.

'Because I disliked you too much and didn't want to help you in any way. I've never forgotten how you spoke to me when you were a child.'

Mrs Reed

How did Jane Eyre speak to her aunt when she was a child? Go back to page 26 if you don't remember.

Do you remember bad things people did to you or can you forgive and forget?

Discuss with a partner.

'I'm sorry, Aunt. I was only a child,' I said.

She wasn't interested in my apology and continued talking.

'I took my revenge on you•. I wrote to your uncle and told him you were dead. There! I have said it. Now do what you want. You were born to be my torment.'

'Don't think about it again, Aunt,' I replied. 'Kiss me and let us forget the past.'

I put my lips near her cheek but she moved her head away. She couldn't love me even now.

'Love me or hate me, then, as you like,' I said at last. 'I forgive you everything. Ask God to do the same and be at peace.'

That night Mrs Reed died.

My plans were to stay at Gateshead only for a week or two but it was a month before I started my journey back to Thornfield.

- **took my revenge on you:** did something bad to you in return for what you did to me

11 Back to Thornfield

I decided to walk to Thornfield Hall from Millcote because I didn't want Mrs Fairfax to send a carriage for me. It wasn't a particularly nice summer evening when I set out but I saw many farmers working in the fields. I felt glad but I wasn't sure why. It wasn't my home that I was going to and I had no real friends there.

'But Mrs Fairfax and Adela will be happy to see you,' I told myself. 'However, you know very well that you're thinking of someone else, and that he isn't thinking of you.'

I was anxious to get to the house as soon as I could so I took the shorter way across the fields. Suddenly there he was! Mr Rochester himself, sitting on a wall with a book and pencil in his hands.

'Jane Eyre,' he said. 'Where have you been? Have you forgotten me?'

'Of course not, sir,' I replied. Why was my body trembling? Why was it so difficult for me to speak?

'Well, hurry home and rest your tired feet,' he said, getting off the wall to let me pass.

I wanted to walk away calmly but something made me stop and turn round.

'Thank you, Mr Rochester,' I said. 'I am strangely glad to get back again to you. Where you are is my home, my only home.'

Then I walked away so fast that Mr Rochester had no possibility of catching up with me.

Everyone at Thornfield Hall was glad to see me and I felt loved. After tea Mrs Fairfax, Adela and I sat together in Mrs Fairfax's room, happy to be in each other's company again.

The weather was beautiful that summer – the sun shone every day. One evening, after putting Adela to bed, I went out into the garden to enjoy the cool air. I soon discovered that I wasn't the only person taking an evening walk.

'Thornfield is a pleasant place in summer, isn't it, Jane?' Mr Rochester said.

'Yes, sir.'

'You must be fond of• the house now. It's a shame• that you must move on•.'

'Must I move on, sir?' I asked. 'Must I leave Thornfield?'

'I really think you must, Jane, because I'm going to get married next month. I've found you a new job in Ireland.'

The news came as a shock. I tried to stay calm but tears started to run silently down my face.

'Ireland is a long way away, sir,' I said.

'It is, Jane, and I'm very sorry I have to send you away. I sometimes have a strange feeling about you – especially when you are near me like now. I feel that there's a string• going from my heart to yours and that it is tied with a tight knot. I feel that if I am separated from you, the string will break and I will be hurt. But you don't feel like this. I think you will forget me.'

'I'll never forget you, sir. But if I have to leave, I will. I love Thornfield. I've never been happier. The thought of never seeing you again fills me with great sadness. But if I have to leave…'

- **a shame:** sad
- **be fond of:** like affectionately
- **move on:** (here) move to another job
- **string:**

'Why do you have to leave?'

'Because of your bride, sir.'

'My bride! What bride? I have no bride!'

'But you will have.'

'Yes. I will!'

'Then I must go. You've told me yourself.'

'No! You must stay,' he said taking me in his arms. I tried to free myself of his embrace but he held me tighter.

'Jane, please don't push me away! You're like a wild frantic• bird that is trying to escape.'

'I'm not a bird and I have no cage or net around me. I am a free person. I can make my own decisions about my life. Now let me go!'

I pulled myself free and stood in front of him.

'Then decide your own destiny,' he said. 'I offer you my hand, my heart, and a share of all my possessions. Marry me, Jane!'

I didn't know what to reply. I thought he was making fun of me.

'Can I believe you?' I said eventually. 'Do you truly love me? Do you sincerely want me to be your wife?'

'I do. I do.'

'Then, sir, I will marry you.'

'Edward! Not "sir", my little wife!'

• **frantic:** very excited

In the morning I wondered if Mr Rochester's proposal was only a dream. To be sure that it wasn't, I needed to hear the words again so after breakfast I went to find him.

'My little Jane Eyre!' he said kissing me. 'Soon to be Jane Rochester!'

At that moment I felt something stronger than joy – I think it was almost fear.

He talked about our wedding, the clothes he wanted to buy me, the places he wanted to take me to, the jewels he wanted to give me.

'I don't want jewels,' I told him. 'But there are two things I want to ask you. The first is: why did you pretend that you wanted to marry Miss Ingram?'

'Because I wanted to make you love me as much as I love you and I know jealousy helps love,' he replied. 'And the second thing?'

'Please talk to Mrs Fairfax about our marriage. She's a good person and I like her very much. I don't want her to have a bad opinion of me.'

Mr Rochester promised and I went to my room. Later I went downstairs to see her.

She looked at me calmly and said, 'I can't believe it. Are you really going to marry him? Does he love you?' she asked.

This hurt me and my eyes filled with tears.

'I'm sorry to upset you,' Mrs Fairfax said. 'But I must warn you to be careful. Things are not always what they seem to be.'

A month passed and my wedding day approached. My trunk was packed and my dress and veil were hanging in the wardrobe.

Then one night while Mr Rochester was away on business, I woke up suddenly after a bad dream. A candle was burning in my room. I looked around and saw a tall female figure near the wardrobe. She was looking at my wedding dress. She took out the veil, put it on and looked at herself in the mirror. Then she pulled it off and tore it into two pieces. I saw her face in the mirror. It was dark and savage! I think I fainted from fear.

The night before our wedding I told Mr Rochester about the woman. It was Grace Poole, he said. I wanted to believe him but I wasn't convinced.

'I can see that you are nervous, Jane,' he said. 'Sleep with Adela tonight and lock the door from the inside.'

I did and I felt safe with my arms around the little girl, but I couldn't sleep.

Early the next morning Sophie helped me put on my wedding dress. I didn't recognise myself when I looked in the mirror before going downstairs.

Mr Rochester was impatient to get to the church and made me walk so fast that I was out of breath when we reached the gate.

The church was very quiet. The only people there were the vicar• and his clerk• and two shadowy• figures in a corner looking at the Rochester tombs. Then the service began. The vicar announced our intention to get married and asked us if there was a reason why we shouldn't.

At that moment, a voice at the back of the church said, 'The marriage cannot take place.'

'Continue!' shouted Mr Rochester angrily.

'I can't continue,' said the vicar, 'until we know what the problem is. Sir, tell us why the marriage cannot take place.'

The speaker came forward. He introduced himself as Mr Briggs, a solicitor• from London.

'Because Mr Rochester is already married,' he said. 'And his wife is still living.'

I looked at Mr Rochester. His face was deathly white•.

- **clerk:** office worker who does administration
- **deathly white:** so white that he looked dead
- **shadowy:** dark; not very visible
- **solicitor:** legal representative
- **vicar:** Anglican priest

'Have you got proof•?' demanded Mr Rochester.

Mr Briggs took a piece of paper out of his pocket and read it to us.

'*I can prove that on the 20th October (then a date fifteen years ago) Edward Rochester married my sister Bertha Antoinetta Mason in Spanish Town, Jamaica. I, myself, have a copy of the marriage certificate. Signed, Richard Mason.*'

Then he said there was a witness• to prove that the lady was still living.

A pale face appeared behind Briggs. It was Mr Mason.

'Can you tell us if Mr Rochester's wife is still living?'

'She is. At Thornfield Hall,' said Mason slowly. 'I saw her there last April. I am her brother.'

'At Thornfield Hall!' exclaimed the vicar. 'Impossible! I've lived here for years, sir, and I've never heard of a Mrs Rochester at Thornfield Hall.'

'That is because I made sure no one heard of it,' said Mr Rochester. 'Come with me, all of you. We'll go to Thornfield Hall and I'll show you my "wife".'

Mr Rochester took my hand and we hurried back to Thornfield. I was again without breath when we arrived, but this time it was because of the shock. The vicar, his clerk, Mr Briggs and Mr Mason followed us.

The 'Wife'

Have you guessed who Mr Rochester's wife is?
How do you think Jane Eyre is feeling at this moment?

- **proof:** something that shows that something is true
- **witness:** person who can say something is true

We all went upstairs to the attic. Grace Poole was sitting near the fire, but she wasn't alone. At one end of the room a figure was running up and down like an animal. It was growling like a dog. When it saw Mr Rochester it stood up and moved the hair that fell over its face. I recognised it at once. The woman who tore my veil! Suddenly she threw herself at Mr Rochester and tried to bite him. She was strong but he managed to hold her arms. Grace Poole helped him tie her to a chair.

'That is my "wife"!' he said. 'Look at her! Then look at the young innocent girl I wanted to marry. Can you blame me for wanting a little happiness? Now go! I must make sure that my real wife is locked safely in.'

e·ZONE ONLINE ACTIVITIES Chapters 8-11

12 Escape

I went to my room and took off my wedding dress. I sat down – tired and weak – and started thinking. Yesterday I was Jane Eyre, almost a bride. I had love and hope. Today I had nothing. I still loved Mr Rochester but I knew I could not stay with him.

It was late afternoon when I finally got up and opened my door. Mr Rochester was sitting on a chair outside my room waiting for me.

'You've come out at last,' he said. 'Jane, will you ever forgive me?'

I forgave him immediately but I didn't tell him.

'Give me your hand, Jane. I want to explain everything. Just listen to me for a few minutes. Please!'

He told me that his father forced him to marry Bertha because her family was rich and his family needed money. He didn't know about her madness until it was too late.

'We can go away,' he continued. 'Away from Thornfield and start a new life.'

'No,' I said. 'I must leave you and Thornfield. I love you more than ever but I can't stay. I must begin a new life. Your wife is still living and I won't be your mistress•.'

Mr Rochester begged• me to stay with him and I wanted to say yes but I couldn't.

I packed my few things in a parcel and left Thornfield. I knew that I had to get as far away as possible from there and the man I loved.

- **begged:** (here) asked in a desperate way
- **mistress:** woman in a romantic relationship with a man married to someone else

Two days later the coach left me at a place called Whitcross. I had no money now and I was completely alone. I started to walk. I walked for a very long time although I was tired and very hungry. Then it started to rain hard. I looked around for shelter• and finally found a small cottage. Through the window I could see two girls with an old lady. I knocked on the door and asked for help but the old lady told me to go away. I was so exhausted that I fell just outside the door, all my hope and strength gone.

'I'm going to die,' I said aloud to myself.

'All men must die,' said a voice in the darkness.

'Who's there?' I asked, terrified.

A man appeared and knocked loudly on the door.

'Is it you, Mr St John•?' asked the old lady inside.

'Yes, yes. Open quickly, Hannah.' Then he said to me, 'Stand up young woman and go in.'

With difficulty I obeyed him. Soon I was sitting in a clean, bright kitchen with a cup of hot milk and some bread in front of me. One of the girls asked my name.

'Jane Elliot,' I replied.

'Are you lost? Can we get in touch with your family or friends?' asked the man.

'I'm alone in the world,' was my answer.

Later they took me upstairs and put me into a warm, dry bed.

- **shelter:** a place giving protection from bad weather or danger
- **St John:** name (here pronounced [sinjin])

For the next three days I slept. I had a fever and couldn't move.

On the fifth day I felt well enough to get up. I slowly and quietly went downstairs to the kitchen to meet the kind people who were looking after me. Hannah, the older lady and servant, was baking bread. She smiled at me and told me to sit by the fire. She began to ask me questions.

'Have you been begging• a long time?' she said.

I was shocked and told her that I wasn't a beggar.

'Why haven't you got a home or money, then?' she asked.

'I'll find a job and a home as soon as I can,' I replied.

Then she told me the two girls, Diana and Mary Rivers, were sisters and the man, St John, was their brother. He was a vicar in the next village.

At that moment they all came in. They greeted me kindly and I thanked them for their hospitality•. They had lots of questions for me too. I explained my situation without giving them too many details.

'I'm not married and I have no home,' I began. 'I was at Lowood School and worked there as a teacher. Then I found a position as a governess. But, a few days ago I had to leave. I can't tell you why. I didn't do anything wrong – I'm not a criminal. Now I must find work and earn my own money again.'

'So you're a teacher?' said St John. 'A new church school for girls is opening here next month. I haven't found a teacher for it yet. The pay will be thirty pounds a year, and there's a cottage for the schoolmistress to live in. Would you like to be this schoolmistress?'

'Thank you, Mr Rivers. Yes, I would, very much,' I replied.

I spent a few more happy weeks with the Rivers and then we all went our different ways – I moved to my cottage, Diana and Mary back to their jobs as governesses and St John to his vicarage•.

- **begging:** (here) asking for food or money as charity
- **hospitality:** kind and welcoming nature
- **vicarage:** house in which a vicar lives

My students at the school were simple village girls and farmers' daughters. I taught them to read, knit, sew and sing. I worked hard and was always busy but I was happy with my job. It was only at night that I remembered my past life. I often imagined meeting Mr Rochester once again.

St John came every day to teach an hour of religion at the school, and during the holidays he came to visit me. On one particular visit he asked to look at my drawings.

I showed them to him with pleasure. He complimented me on my skill• as he turned over the sheets• of paper. Then suddenly he stopped. He was looking at the blank• sheet I rested my hand on while painting. I don't know what he saw on it but he got up quickly, said goodbye and left.

- **blank:** empty
- **sheets:** pages
- **skill:** talent; ability

13 A New Life

8 The next day St John came back.

'I want to have a little talk with you,' he said. 'Come and sit with me near the fire.'

When we were both seated, he took an envelope out of his pocket and held it up.

'A few weeks ago I received this letter from a Mr Briggs in London,' he said. 'It contains details of a girl called Jane Eyre. Yesterday I saw that name on a piece of paper among your drawings. You aren't Jane Elliot, are you? You are Jane Eyre.'

'Mr Rivers, does the letter mention Mr Rochester?' was all I could think of to say.

'No,' he replied. 'Mr Briggs wants to find Jane Eyre because he has something important to tell her. He put an advertisement in the newspapers and a Mrs Fairfax saw it and wrote to him. She gave him the details. Mr Briggs wants to tell you that your uncle, Mr Eyre of Madeira, has died and left you all his money. You are a rich woman now.'

'Me! Rich?'

'Yes. You have twenty thousand pounds.'

I looked at him in astonishment•.

'But, tell me,' I said when I found my voice. 'Why did Mr Briggs write to you about me?'

'My mother's name was Eyre. She had two brothers – one who married Miss Jane Reed of Gateshead and John Eyre who went to Madeira. Mr Briggs was Mr Eyre's solicitor. He contacted us when he couldn't find you.'

• **astonishment:** shock

'So your mother was my father's sister?'

'Yes.'

'And therefore my aunt?'

He nodded.

'So you three, Diana, Mary and yourself, are my cousins?'

'Yes!'

I clapped my hands with joy! I had a family, people I could love and who were kind to me. I was no longer alone.

'I am so, so glad!'

'You are happier to hear you have cousins than to hear you have a fortune.'

'Of course! Before I was alone and now I have a family. Write to Diana and Mary tomorrow and tell them to come home. With my money they will no longer have to work.'

Family

With a friend draw Jane's family tree.

Do you think having a family is important? Why?

I decided to share the twenty thousand pounds between the four of us. I gave up my teaching job at the school and moved back to the cottage to live with my cousins, Diana and Mary. St John still lived at the vicarage but he often visited us. This was a happy time for me.

One day St John told us that he was going to India to work as a missionary•. He started learning Hindustani and asked me to help him. I agreed and after that we spent many hours studying together. As I got to know him better, I realised that he was a very serious person.

• **missionary:** person in a foreign land teaching Christianity

He was also very difficult to please.

I still thought about Mr Rochester a lot. I knew I couldn't visit him but I wanted to know how he was. I decided to write to Mrs Fairfax. Two months passed without a reply. I wrote again. Day after day the post arrived but there was never anything for me. This upset me greatly.

Summer came and one sunny morning St John invited me to go for a walk. While we were resting on a rock, he asked me to marry him and go with him to India.

I said no straightaway, perhaps too quickly. I didn't love St John and I don't believe he really loved me. He just wanted me to help him with his missionary work.

I knew that my heart still belonged to Mr Rochester. I desperately wanted news of him so I decided to go to Thornfield and find out for myself how he was.

I told my cousins I was going away for a few days. They didn't ask me where.

I took a coach most of the way and then walked the last two miles to Thornfield. I walked quickly, sometimes even running. I was happy to see the woods again but most of all I couldn't wait to see Mr Rochester's face.

I finally arrived at the wall that surrounded the garden. I turned the corner, anxious to see the house. I expected to see Thornfield Hall in all its glory. Instead I saw a ruin•.

The front of the house was still there. But there was no roof. There were no chimneys, no windows. There was the silence of death there. I understood now why I received no replies to my letters.

What caused this disaster? Did anyone die?

There was no one here to answer these questions. No clue• to explain the disaster.

• **clue:** fact that helps solve a mystery or problem • **ruin:** building in a very bad state

The disaster

Can you answer Jane's questions? What do you think happened at Thornfield Hall?

The innkeeper of a local inn• eventually told me the story.

'It happened last autumn,' he said. 'After the governess disappeared (but that's another story), Mr Rochester sent his housekeeper and Miss Adela away and shut himself up at the Hall. Then one night a fire broke out. They say it was started by a mad woman who lived in the attic. This woman was later discovered to be Mr Rochester's wife. She managed to set fire to her own room and also to one of the bedrooms on the next floor. Luckily all the servants got out in time but the mad woman went up on the roof. Mr Rochester tried to save her but she jumped off and fell to her death.'

'Were there any other deaths?' I asked.

'No,' he replied. 'But poor Mr Rochester...'

'What about him?' I asked, dreading• his answer.

'Mr Rochester suffers greatly. A piece of burning wood fell on him and he was badly hurt. He was rescued but he's now blind.'

'Where is he? Where does he live now?'

'In a house on one of his farms about thirty miles away. Old John and his wife look after him.'

'Will you take me there? I'll pay you well.'

'With pleasure, ma'am. And on the way I'll tell you the story of the governess.'

'There's no need,' I replied. 'I know that story already.'

When we were a mile from the house, I paid the innkeeper and sent him back. I wanted to arrive on foot.

It was early evening and the only sound I could hear was the rain on the leaves.

'Can there be life here?' I asked myself as I approached the house.

Yes, there was. I heard a movement and a figure came out into the evening light and stood on the step. It was a man without a hat. He put his hand out to feel the rain. It was my master, Edward Rochester!

• **dreading:** fearing greatly

• **inn:** small hotel

Blindness

Discuss with a partner and then with the class.

Imagine what it is like to be blind.
Write a list of all the difficulties a blind person has in everyday life.

I stopped and watched him. I wanted to observe him. He couldn't see me of course because he was blind.

Physically, he looked the same as a year ago. He was still a strong man. His back was still straight. His hair was still black. But in his face I could see desperation. He took a few uncertain steps, putting out his arms in front of him to feel his way. Then, defeated, he turned and went back into the house.

I waited for a while and then I knocked on the door. Mary, an old servant from Thornfield Hall, opened it. She couldn't believe her eyes when she saw me. I took her hand and followed her into the kitchen. I explained everything to her while we were sitting next to the fire. Then a bell rang. It was Mr Rochester. He wanted some water.

'Give the tray to me,' I said. 'I'll take it to him.'

I was shaking as I went in and my heart was beating fast.

Mr Rochester turned around when he heard the door opening. But because he saw nothing, he turned back and sighed.

I approached him with the glass of water.

'It is you, Mary, isn't it?'

'Mary's in the kitchen,' I said.

'Who is this? Who is this?' he demanded. 'Answer me! Speak again!' he ordered.

'I arrived only this evening,' I said.

'That voice! It's hers! Have I gone mad? Come here! Let me touch you.'

I put my hand in his.

'They're her fingers!' he cried. Then he felt my shoulders, my neck, my waist. 'Yes! It's her shape, her size. Jane!'

'My dear master,' I answered, 'I've found you. I've come back to you. I'll never leave you again.'

I put my arms around him and kissed his poor eyes. Then I told him about my new family and my fortune and explained why I went back to Thornfield and how I knew about the fire.

14 Conclusion

9 Reader, I married him. We had a quiet but beautiful wedding.

I wrote and told my cousins about it. Diana and Mary were happy for us but St John didn't reply.

I went to see Adela at her school. She was so pleased to see me again. She looked thin and pale and I discovered that the teachers there were very strict. I decided to take her away and put her in another school closer to us. Her new teachers are much kinder and she's doing well in her studies now. We often go and visit her.

I have been married for ten years. I live for my husband and he for me. We talk all day long and never get tired of each other. We are perfectly suited and so live together in complete harmony.

For the first two years of our marriage I was Edward's eyes. He saw everything through me. Then one day he told me he could see a little. Following the advice of a doctor in London, he eventually recovered the sight in one eye. It isn't perfect but good enough for him to find his way around. When I put our first baby in his arms, he could see that the child had his eyes – as they were before the fire – large, brilliant and black.

My Edward and I are very happy together. And the happiness of the people we love most makes us even happier.

e-ZONE ONLINE ACTIVITIES Chapters 12-14

AFTER READING TALK ABOUT THE BOOK

1 Answer the questions.

a Did you enjoy reading the story? Why/Why not?

b Who was your favourite character? Why?

c Do you think Jane Eyre is passionate and courageous? Why/Why not?

d What kind of hero do you think Mr Rochester is?

e Did you guess Mr Rochester was already married to Bertha? Or was it a big surprise?

f Do you think the ending is realistic? Would you change it? How?

2 *Jane Eyre* was an immediate success when it was published in 1847 but it created a scandal. Can you think why? Consider the following then discuss with a partner:

a a poor girl rebels against her guardian;

b a young girl advertises for a new job;

c a governess falls in love with her employer;

d a married man wants to marry another woman;

e the story is written in the first-person narrative.

AFTER READING COMPREHENSION

1 Tick (✓) true (T) or false (F).

		T	F
a	Jane Eyre enjoyed her childhood at Gateshead Hall and was sad to leave.	☐	☐
b	Lowood was an institution where most of the girls were orphans.	☐	☐
c	Mr Brocklehurst humiliated Jane but Miss Temple was kind to her.	☐	☐
d	Lowood didn't really change while Jane was there.	☐	☐
e	Jane met her employer on the day she arrived at Thornfield Hall.	☐	☐
f	Jane disliked Mr Rochester at first but she thought he was very handsome.	☐	☐
g	Mr Rochester asked Jane not to talk to the servants about the fire in his room.	☐	☐
h	Jane knew about and understood the mystery at Thornfield Hall early on in the story.	☐	☐
i	Mr Mason stayed at Thornfield Hall for less than 24 hours.	☐	☐
j	Mr Rochester was very relaxed on the morning of his wedding to Jane.	☐	☐
k	Mr Rochester was forced to marry Bertha by his father – he didn't know she was mad.	☐	☐
l	Jane heard about Mr Rochester and his blindness from Mrs Fairfax.	☐	☐

2 **Correct the false sentences in Exercise 1.**

3 **Match the two parts of the sentences.**

a ☐ Jane tried hard to be good for her aunt but

b ☐ Miss Temple helped Jane clear her name at Lowood because

c ☐ Jane often heard a strange laugh at Thornfield but

d ☐ Mr Rochester pretended he wanted to marry Miss Ingram in order

1 she didn't learn the truth about it until much later.

2 nothing she did satisfied Mrs Reed.

3 to make Jane jealous and love him more.

4 she wrote to Mr Lloyd to ask him about Jane.

4 **Work with a partner and explain why the following are important to the story.**

a

b

c

AFTER READING CHARACTERS

1 Tick the words which can be used to describe Jane.

☐ deceitful	☐ honest	☐ daring
☐ plain	☐ cruel	☐ courageous
☐ stern	☐ sincere	☐ strong

2 In the course of the story the reader witnesses Jane Eyre's growth in character from an unhappy lonely child to a strong young woman. Put the following stages of the development of Jane's character into the correct order.

a ☐ Jane is wrongly accused by Mr Brocklehurst and she wants to clear her name.

b ☐ Jane tells her aunt, Mrs Reed, what she thinks of her.

c ☐ Jane forgives Mrs Reed before she dies.

d ☐ Jane studies and works hard at Lowood and eventually becomes a teacher.

e ☐ Jane fights back at her cousin's bullying.

f ☐ Jane refuses to marry St John because she does not love him.

g ☐ Jane is strong and is able to play Mr Rochester's game when he provokes her.

h ☐ Jane loves Mr Rochester but will not stay with him if she cannot be his wife.

i ☐ Jane finds her first job as a governess without anyone's help.

j ☐ Jane goes back to Mr Rochester when she hears he is blind and is now a free man.

k ☐ Jane makes good progress with her pupil Adela.

l ☐ Jane falls in love with Mr Rochester.

3 Complete this paragraph about Mr Rochester with the words in the box.

hero	women	fire
character	element	love

Mr Rochester is an important **a** .... in the story. He is not your typical romantic **b** .... He is not handsome and is often moody. This makes him a mysterious character. He is fascinating to **c** ...., as we see with Blanche Ingram and Jane Eyre. He is kind to Adela and to his mad wife, Bertha (he never wants to hurt her and tries to save her in the **d** .... at the end of the story). We see that he is capable of great **e** .... through his feelings for and relationship with Jane Eyre. Mr Rochester is an essential **f** .... in this powerful love story.

4 Put the characters into the correct column.

Mr Brocklehurst   Mrs Fairfax   Diana Rivers
John Reed   Mr Mason   Miss Temple   Blanche Ingram
Bessie   Grace Poole   Mary Rivers   Adela   Helen Burns
Aunt Reed   Bertha   St John Rivers   Mr Rochester

GATESHEAD HALL	LOWOOD INSTITUTION	THORNFIELD HALL	COTTAGE NEAR WHITCROSS
....	....	....	....
....	....	....	....
....	....	....	....
....	....	....	....
....	....	....	....
....	....	....	....
....	....	....	....

NEW

AFTER READING VOCABULARY

1 Complete, where possible, the word formation table below with words taken from the text.

NOUN	ADJECTIVE	ADVERB
MADNESS	MAD	MADLY
....	CAREFUL	....
	GOOD	....
ANXIETY	....	....
....	HUMBLE	....
....	....	HARD
....	WARM	....
RUDENESS	....	RUDELY
	FAST	....
WIDTH	....	....
....	WISE	WISELY
QUIET	....	....
....	STRONG	....
WOOD	....	
....	ALIVE	
....	KIND	....

2 Complete the sentences with words from Exercise 1.

a 'We will teach Miss Eyre .... and obedience.'

b I tried .... to be good but nothing I did was good enough for my aunt.

c Girls of all ages were sitting on .... benches on each side of long tables.

d Helen's smile gave me .... and I stood on my stool with my head up high.

e That evening we feasted on food, ..., kindness and affection.

f 'She's treating me like a visitor,' I thought, 'I wasn't expecting such .... from an employer.

3 For each of the sentences below, write a new sentence as similar as possible in meaning to the original one but using the words given in capitals; do not change these words in any way.

a She took me to a small comfortable room with a cheerful fire.
WAS

b I had no reason to complain about my life at Thornfield Hall.
ANY

c For the next few days I saw little of Mr Rochester. He was always busy. **MUCH**

d I walked away so fast that Mr Rochester had no possibility of catching up with me. **CATCH**

e With my money they will no longer have to work. **ANYMORE**

4 Use five of the words in the box to complete the sentences.

rumour	conscious	bars	carriage
witness	lack	attitude	bachelor

a If you .... something, it means you don't have it.

b A .... is a four-wheel horse-drawn vehicle.

c .... means awake and able to think.

d .... in prison cell windows are to prevent people from getting out.

e An unmarried man is also called a ....

5 In pairs, create three sentences with the words left out in Exercise 4.

AFTER READING LANGUAGE

1 Complete the sentences with the correct form of *make/let*.

a Finally he gave me some of my wages and .... me promise to return.

b I was determined not to .... her upset me.

c This .... me cry even harder.

d I wanted to walk away calmly but something .... me stop and turn round.

e Mr Rochester was impatient to get to the church and .... me walk so fast that I was out of breath when we reached the gate

f Helen .... me feel calm.

g He got off the wall to .... me pass.

2 Bertha Rochester spent most of her adult life locked in an attic, but she does have a big impact on the story and the characters. Make a list of all the things Bertha Rochester *managed* to do before she died.

Bertha Rochester

She managed to set fire to her own room and also to one of the bedrooms on the next floor.

....

....

....

....

3 **Write and then answer questions in the past using How long...? about the following.**

a Jane Eyre / live/ at Gateshead Hall
How long .... ?
....

b Jane Eyre / stay / at Lowood
How long .... ?
....

c Jane Eyre / stand / on a stool
How long .... ?
....

d Jane Eyre / stay / at Gateshead / Aunt Reed's death
How long .... ?
....

e Jane Eyre / engaged / to Mr Rochester
How long .... ?
....

4 **Write questions and answers about the following characters using Why... *because*. Use the adjectives in the box.**

sincere	cruel	strange	wicked
humble	obedient	honest	complicated

a

b

c

d

AFTER READING PLOT AND THEME

1 **Jane Eyre and her story have strong signs of early feminism. Put the following in the correct order. Then, with a partner, find each episode in the book, and prepare a question and answer session with Jane Eyre about at least two of them.**

- **a** ☐ Jane advertises and finds her first job as a governess with a good salary.
- **b** ☐ Jane returns to Mr Rochester when she is his independent equal – she has her own money and is no longer in his employment.
- **c** ☐ Jane wants to be independent and is happy to find a new job when she leaves Thornfield Hall.
- **d** ☐ Jane will not become Mr Rochester's mistress.
- **e** ☐ Jane studies and works hard to become a governess.

2 **Match the different motivations behind these relationships to the couples.**

- **a** ☐ Jane Eyre and Mr Rochester
- **b** ☐ Mr Rochester and Blanche Ingram
- **c** ☐ Mr Rochester and Bertha Rochester
- **d** ☐ Jane Eyre and St John Rivers

1 help with missionary work
2 love
3 political or social union
4 money

3 **Forgiveness is an important theme in the story. Write down examples of how these characters show signs of forgiveness.**

Helen Burns	
Mr Rochester	
Jane Eyre	

4 **At the beginning of the story Jane Eyre is a lonely orphan living with cousins who hate her, but by the end Jane's wish for a loving family comes true and she finds some more cousins. Look at this family tree for Jane Eyre. Underline the characters who actually appear in the story.**

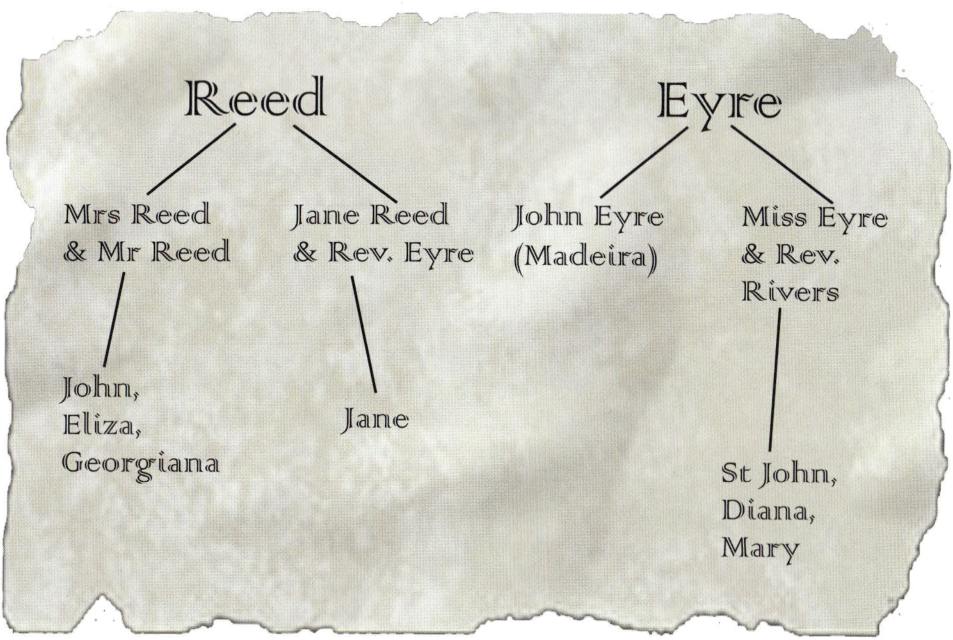

Cinderella Stories?

Jane Eyre has often been compared to the fairy tale of *Cinderella*. At the time Brontë's novel was published, two versions of *Cinderella* were immensely popular, namely the **Grimms'** one which was published in 1812 and the version by **Charles Perrault** dating from 1697.

Indeed, the two works share some features•: from the characters' personality traits• to the basic plot, along with some other classic fairy tale clichés•. Brontë's novel offers of course more complex characters and includes religious symbolism that the fairy tale lacks•. And in the relationship between the main characters in *Cinderella* we find no trace• of the conflicts that Brontë's characters are faced with.

Jane and Cinderella

Both heroines are orphans, they both experience lack of love, rejection and exclusion from their families or guardians. The way both couples of lovers fall in love is similar, they both separate and then look for each other (Prince Charming finds Cinderella and Jane finds Mr Rochester) before the happy ending. Both Jane and Cinderella live in societies that dictate a precise code of behaviour for women and offer social status based on nobility and wealth. But there is one big difference, Cinderella is passive and pious•, the perfect role model in Victorian society, while Jane fights conventions and takes an active role in her own destiny.

- **Byronic:** (here) dark, mysterious and often tormented
- **clichés:** ideas that are used so much that they lose some of their original force and meaning
- **features:** important or interesting things
- **lacks:** (here) doesn't have
- **pious:** very religious and dedicated
- **trace:** sign; clue
- **traits:** qualities

No Prince Charming

Although both Prince Charming and Mr Rochester actively search for true love, that is where the similarity ends. The Prince is a model of beauty and perfection, whereas Rochester reminds us much more of Byronic• heroes and perhaps the Beast in *Beauty and the Beast*.

Ultimately, even if there are elements of the Cinderella story in Jane *Eyre*, Brontë's novel cannot really be thought of simply as a variation of Cinderella. The similarities in plot and characters are due to the universal value of the issues involved in the two stories.

The oldest version of the story of Cinderella is around two thousand years old and comes from the Greek geographer **Strabo**. He wrote about a young slave girl who eventually married the king of Egypt.

In pairs think of as many books, films and songs as you can that contain elements of the Cinderella story.

NEW

AFTER READING CAMBRIDGE ENGLISH EXAMS

P Preparation for Preliminary English Test (PET) Reading Part 5

1 Complete the sentences below by choosing the correct answer.

a Neither of us said ..... .
A nothing **B** something **C** anything **D** thing

b We have to ..... the house ready for the arrival of the guests.
A make **B** let **C** turn **D** get

c - Blanche is the most beautiful of all.
- What ..... she like?
A has **B** looks **C** seems **D** is

d The vicar announced our intention to get married and asked us if there was a reason why we ..... .
A must **B** wanted **C** shouldn't **D** married

e Day after day the post arrived but there was never ..... for me.
A anything **B** something **C** nothing **D** letters

f Some girls were sent home ..... to escape the fever or to die.
A either **B** also **C** or **D** if

g Edward recovered the sight in one eye. It isn't perfect but good enough for him to find his way ..... .
A in **B** out **C** around **D** soon

h The beautiful lady ..... Mrs Fairfax's description of Blanche Ingram.
A matched **B** seemed **C** looked **D** could

i I went to a village to post a letter. I was nearly ..... there when I heard the sound of a horse galloping at great speed.
A in **B** halfway **C** arrived **D** got

j Only Bessie was nice to me and I preferred her to ..... else.
A no one **B** anyone **C** one **D** someone

l I'm sorry to upset you, but I ..... warn you to be careful.
A could **B** can **C** might **D** must

P Preparation for Preliminary English Test (PET) Reading Part 6

2 Complete the text about Charlotte Brontë by choosing one word for each space.

When she was fifteen, Charlotte Brontë **(1)**......... sent as a pupil to Miss Wooler's school at Roe Head. She was shy and conscious of her unattractive appearance and social embarrassment. At first, her lack of beauty, fashion, and social graces made her feel **(2)**......... of place. But in time she won the respect and affection of those around her and began to feel at home in the school. Although her father's social position as clergyman allowed them to be members of the upper-middle class, the Brontës were not real gentry, due **(3)**......... their economic status; and the three sisters had few prospects for the future. So, at one time or another, they all had to work **(4)**......... governesses, and they all disliked the work. At that time, governesses **(5)**......... regarded in most households as little more than servants. Like teachers, they were very poorly paid, worked very **(6)**......... hours in spite **(7)**......... their education and class origins that were often similar to those of their employers. And once the children reached a certain age, governesses would become redundant and would be obliged to leave. But no other way to independence was open to **(8)**......... .

P Preparation for Preliminary English Test (PET) Writing Part 2

3 Imagine you are Jane Eyre. Write an email of about 50 words in reply to the following message received by Mr Briggs about the money you have received.

Send

From: Mr Briggs
To: Ms Jane Eyre

Dear Ms Eyre,
It seems to me that you are happier to read you have a family than to read you have a fortune! Why?

AFTER READING EXIT TEST

1 MP3 **Listen and tick (✓) the correct picture.**

a 1 

2 

b 1 

2 

c 1 

2 

d 1 

2 

2 **P** **Tick (✓) true (T) or false (F).**

		T	F
a	Bessie is the only person who is nice to Jane Eyre at Gateshead Hall.	☐	☐
b	Mr Brocklehurst makes Jane Eyre stand on a chair at the back of the classroom.	☐	☐
c	Grace Poole does the cooking and other jobs at Thornfield Hall.	☐	☐
d	Mr Rochester is really happy to see Mr Mason.	☐	☐
e	Jane Eyre sees Bertha Rochester twice when she is at Thornfield Hall.	☐	☐
f	St John Rivers helps Jane find a job as a teacher.	☐	☐
g	Jane Eyre divides her fortune with her cousins St John, Diana and Mary.	☐	☐
h	Jane Eyre meets Mr Rochester again at Thornfield Hall.	☐	☐

3 **Correct the false sentences.**

4 **P** **Imagine you are Jane Eyre. You are happy to have found Mr Rochester again.**

Write a letter to your cousins Diana and Mary Rivers. In your letter, you should:

- tell Diana and Mary about your journey to Thornfield Hall;
- say what the innkeeper told you about the disaster;
- say where you are now;
- ask Diana and Mary to visit you.

Write 35-45 words.

e·ZONE ONLINE ACTIVITIES After Reading

AFTER READING PROJECT

Wide Sargasso Sea

The novelist Jean Rhys (1890-1979) retold Jane Eyre's story through the character Bertha Rochester (renamed Antoinette) in her novel *Wide Sargasso Sea* (1966).

In groups of four do some research on the Internet or in a library about *Wide Sargasso Sea* and its connection to *Jane Eyre*. Find information about:

- the novelist Jean Rhys – her life and her reasons for writing the novel;
- when and where the novel is set;
- from whose point of view the novel is told (who and how many narrators there are);
- how the novel is connected to *Jane Eyre*.

Then make a poster to illustrate your research and:

- find some images (photos, paintings or designs) that you think might represent the novel;
- find some images for *Jane Eyre* and then state how the images for the two books are different;
- state how, after your research, your original opinion of Bertha and Mr Rochester in *Jane Eyre* has changed.